MW01601184

TESTIMONIALS

"For ages, God's people have turned to scriptures and spiritual writings that speak words of consolation. Reflections from God invites us to do just this: to deeply listen to God's word; to renew ourselves with daily prayer and contemplation; to hear the voice of hope in our days. Enjoy this collection of encouraging verses, selected from the prayer life and faith-filled journey of the author."

Carla Orlando

Spiritual Direction Services Ignatian Spirituality Center, Coordinator

Seattle Pacific University, Instructor

"Do you desire to spend time using scripture verses to understand how God is speaking to you each day? If you do, this book offers you samples to stimulate your own wisdom in applying how God is speaking to you. The twelve themes chosen by Karen Smith will fortify you in your spiritual journey and increase your desire to pray daily. God is speaking directly to you.

Lucy Wynkoop, OSB

Co-author with Christine Valters Paintner of Lectio Divina: Contemplative Awakening and Awareness

"Reflections from God is a beautiful and much needed book. It shows the author's deep love of the Bible and her deep, prayerful engagement with Scripture over the years. In reading and praying with this devotional you will explore a treasury of some of the most inspiring verses in the Bible. And more importantly you will learn how to read the Bible prayerfully, listening for the Word of God. You will learn how God can speak to you personally through Scripture. Keep this lovely book handy, on your night stand or your coffee table, as a source of daily hope and inspiration."

Paul Rietmann, author of Jesus and Buddha Meet in Stillness: A Beginner's Guide to Mindfulness Meditation and Contemplative Prayer

REFLECTIONS FROM GOD

365 BIBLE VERSES FOR
EVERY DAY OF THE YEAR

~ALONG WITH~

DAILY CONTEMPLATIVE REFLECTIONS TO
INSPIRE, GUIDE, AND BRING HOPE

Karen Smith

BookLocker
Trenton, Georgia

Print ISBN: 979-8-88531-177-9
Ebook ISBN: 979-8-88531-178-6

Published by BookLocker.com, Inc., Trenton, Georgia.

Printed on acid-free paper.

BookLocker.com, Inc.
2022

First Edition

Front Cover Photo Credit
Amy Curran

Library of Congress Cataloguing in Publication Data
Smith, Karen
Reflections From God by Karen Smith
Library of Congress Control Number: 2022906799

Back Cover: © AdobeStock_SemilirBanyu (texture abstract);
© AdobeStock.com_CaptureAndCompose (frame)

DISCLAIMER

This book details the author's personal experiences with and opinions about the Bible. The author is not a licensed therapist.

The author and publisher are providing this book and its contents on an "as is" basis and make no representations or warranties of any kind with respect to this book or its contents. The author and publisher disclaim all such representations and warranties, including for example warranties of merchantability and personal advice for a particular purpose. In addition, the author and publisher do not represent or warrant that the information accessible via this book is accurate, complete or current.

The statements made about products and services have not been evaluated by the U.S. government. Please consult with your own legal, accounting, medical, or other licensed professional regarding the suggestions and recommendations made in this book.

Except as specifically stated in this book, neither the author or publisher, nor any authors, contributors, or other representatives will be liable for damages arising out of or in connection with the use of this book. This is a comprehensive limitation of liability that applies to all damages of any kind, including (without limitation) compensatory; direct, indirect or consequential damages; loss of data, income or profit; loss of or damage to property and claims of third parties.

You understand that this book is not intended as a substitute for consultation with a licensed medical, legal or accounting professional. Before you begin any change your lifestyle in any way, you will consult a licensed professional to ensure that you are doing what's best for your situation.

This book provides content related to Biblical topics. As such, use of this book implies your acceptance of this disclaimer.

ACKNOWLEDGMENTS

First and foremost, I thank God who led me on this spirit filled journey and leads me every day with His love, and for this I am grateful.

Also, there have been a handful of people who have accompanied me on the road to writing this devotional, that I would like to acknowledge. First of all, my two children Caitlin and Cole, who always give me their love and support in all areas of my life, and for the love and laughter we share through it all, I thank you. For my father and mother who gave me both a firm foundation of faith, and knowing the love of God and Jesus, I am thankful. For my Divine Women of Faith, you know who you are, you lit my path with your light and love, and kept me moving forward, and for that I am thankful. For my spiritual mentors, Neill, Paul, and Father Colin, you, by your love and care for others, remind me that Jesus still walks on this earth today through us, I thank you. And last but not least for Christie, who led me through this process, in kindness, to getting it done, thank you.

INTRODUCTION

My love of the Bible started in my mid-twenties when I participated in a five-year course through an organization called Bible Study Fellowship, which explored different books of the Bible. I immensely enjoyed reading for the course—and at the same time, I found great comfort and peace reading the Bible at night. It quickly became one of my favorite bedside table books. The Bible continues to be a book that guides my days and nights with wisdom, inspiration, and hope.

One day, shortly after starting Bible Study Fellowship, I purchased a small leather notebook with the intention of writing a daily journal. That idea never came to fruition; God had different plans for that leather notebook. Another idea came to mind and I started to write down my favorite Bible verses to have and reflect upon, a practice that began eight years ago.

~

I continued to grow deeply in my faith, getting involved with a contemplative meditation practice called Contemplative Prayer. This practice, derived from ancient monks and inspired by Jesus, calls for followers to sit with God in silence. Contemplative Prayer helps to open and consent to God's presence and action within us. Consequentially we develop a loving relationship with God and feel God's Divine love. As I sat in stillness and emptied myself of the cares and distractions of the world, I grew deep in communion with God. It is a wonderful practice, one that has become an important part of my life.

A few years later, I connected with a woman in my Contemplative Prayer group who taught me a spiritual practice called Lectio Divina. In this practice, one chooses a passage of the Bible and follows with four actions: Read, Reflect, Respond, and Rest.

I welcomed the mornings with a short Bible passage, and I would carry a verse or verses in my heart throughout the day. Some days, a particular incident would illustrate a direct unfolding of the verse; mostly, it was God speaking to me in my heart. I would respond and rest with the passage at night and write down my reflections. It was this ritual that led me to reflect and ultimately write one for every day of the year.

One evening, as I was writing, I realized the practice of Contemplative Prayer had opened my heart to God's love in my inmost being. Lectio Divina had given me a method to reflect upon and hold these verses. As a result of these two practices, my reflections had become a true gift and blessing from God.

It was then I heard God's quiet whisper in my heart and soul, telling me: "These are not just for you anymore. These need to be shared with others." It was not just a thought, but a loving command.

~

Years passed and my life looked so much different. No longer married, and proudly watching my kids launch their adult lives in other cities, I decided to sell our family home and move to the bustling core of Seattle, leaving behind the quiet island where I had both grown up and raised a family. I then embarked on a two-year course to become a Spiritual Director, under the wise teachings of the Benedictine Sisters at the Priory in Washington.

Impossible to predict was that an even greater change would come: a global pandemic. There was much fear and uncertainty, and how we did just about everything changed. The one thing that remained constant for me, was writing down verses in that small leather journal. In that time of quiet stillness, and being alone, I gained a deeper openness to God. There was no noise to drown out His voice. Is this part of what God was trying to tell us, to listen and be still? Would out of this new life come a renewed understanding of ourselves, our world, and how we were living? As I continued to collect verses and reflect upon the Bible, I came upon a verse that was quite significant to me.

> "For everything that was written in the past was written to teach us, so that through the endurance taught in Scriptures and the encouragement they provide we might have hope."

> Romans 15:4

That verse affirmed to me why I was writing this devotional: so that through the teachings and words of the Bible, we can be inspired, guided, and have hope. Here I was, in a new age, resonating with a verse thousands of years old. Every unexpected turn of my lifetime has brought me back to the everlasting truths in the Bible.

~

Reflections from God came to me through God so that I may share it with you. These hand-selected verses are steeped in traditional values, yet relate to the contemporary world, centered around twelve timeless themes: Love, Joy, Hope, Trust, Faith, Obedience, Humility, Fortitude, Peace, Protection, Knowledge, and Guidance.

Some themes may be easier to sit with, like love and joy; others may be more challenging, like fortitude and trust. Reading these Bible verses daily is a way to grow in knowledge and understanding of God's word; they are a window into God's heart. However you respond to the verses, open yourself to what God is trying to tell you, and in stillness, you may hear it.

We are all simply human, taking this life one day at a time in God's grace and mercy, and He will meet us where we are in our journey. God gave us these Bible verses so that we may get through the complicated times, whether in our most difficult seasons or our most joyous milestones. Life is beautiful in all its complexity and simplicity, if each day is taken with the Creator of it all.

VERSES

January 1

Romans 15:4

For everything that was written in the past was written to teach us, so that through the endurance taught in the Scriptures and the encouragement they provide we might have hope.

Hope

The Scriptures teach us, guide us, and bless us, for they instruct how to live, grow, and face challenges in our lives. The words that have come down through the ages teach us not only how to live in this world, but how to thrive in this world. They give us hope, love, and so much more—a true gift from God.

January 2

2 Peter 1:5-9

For this very reason make every effort to add to your faith goodness: and to goodness knowledge, and to knowledge, self-control; and to self-control perseverance; and to perseverance, godliness; and to godliness brotherly kindness, and to brotherly kindness, love. For if you possess these qualities in increasing measure, they will keep you from being ineffective and unproductive in your knowledge in our Lord Jesus Christ.

Faith

Faith is not only knowing the Lord, but growing in the Lord. When we grow in faith, goodness, self-control, and perseverance, we are getting to know Jesus and all that he wants for us. Walking through this life with these qualities means walking through this life as someone continually seeking Jesus.

January 3

Matthew 6:33

But seek first His kingdom and His righteousness and all these things will be given to you as well.

Obedience

God wants you to put Him before all else. He knows what you need better than you do, and when you seek Him first you are seeking what is truly important. His love, grace, and goodness are all you need, and all your desires will follow. Seek Him first, and let the rest of this life on earth unfold into the beautiful life He has in store for you.

January 4

Galatians 5:22-23

The Fruit of the Spirit is love, joy, peace, patience, kindness, goodness, faithfulness, gentleness and self-control.

Love

The fruit of the Spirit comes from living with God. These fruits in our lives maintain us living in God's constant love. Through living a life with Him in prayer and love, all these wonderful fruits start becoming apparent in our lives, and out of their abundance we can bless those around us.

January 5

John 4:18

There is no fear in love but perfect love casts out fear.

Love

We need to live and move from a place of love, not fear. It is God's way, a peaceful and joyous way. How do we overcome fear and doubts in our lives? We fill our hearts with so much love that there is absolutely no room for fear. Be in constant prayer and thanksgiving for God's love, for it is the ultimate blessing.

January 6

John 14:23

Jesus replied, anyone who loves me will keep my word, and my Father will love him, and we shall come to him and make a home in him.

Obedience

Listening to and following God's teachings is essential to our being. The Lord wants to come to us, to live in us and to make His home in us, but most of all He wants to love us. He created us so we are all worthy of His love, and wants to bless us abundantly with it.

January 7

Psalm 63:1-8

Oh God, you are my God earnestly I seek you; my soul thirsts for you, my body longs for you, in a dry and weary land where there is no water.

I have seen you in the sanctuary and beheld your power and glory.

Because your love is better than life, my lips will glorify you. I will praise you as long as I live, and in your name I will lift up my hands.

My soul will be satisfied as with the richest of foods. With singing lips my mouth will praise you

On my bed I remember you; I think of you through the watches of the night

Because you are my help I sing in the shadows of your wings.

My soul clings to you; your right hand upholds me.

Protection

God watches over us day and night, and for this we are grateful. We need to do our part to move through life safely, but we also need to know God is our protector and guide. We must do our part, but we also need to turn it over to Him, and trust He will do His.

January 8

Philippians 4:4-7

Rejoice in the Lord always, I will say it again: Rejoice!

Let your gentleness be evident to all. The Lord is near. Do not be anxious about anything, but in everything by prayer and petition, with thanksgiving, present your request to God. And the peace of God, which transcends all understanding, will guard your hearts and minds in Christ Jesus.

Peace

The peace that God gives us is like no other. We can worry and fret, or give it over to God and rest in His perfect peace and understanding. Choose God and you choose a life of peace.

January 9

Hebrews 13:5-6

Never will I leave you, never will I forsake you.

So we say with confidence,

"The Lord is my helper, I will not be afraid."

Trust

We can be confident that God is there for us in difficult and challenging times. We are His children and He is our helper. He is always there by our side, so never fear, He is in our midst.

January 10

Psalm 16: 11

You make known to me the path of life;

You will fill me with joy in your presence, with eternal pleasures at your right hand

Guidance

God guides us to a full, abundant life, and if we say yes to all that He has prepared for us, it will be joyful and rich. Along with walking on that path, stop and listen. There are times God will instruct you, but also times He just wants to fill you with His joy and love.

January 11

2 Timothy 1:17

For God did not give us a spirit of timidity, but a spirit of power, of love and self-control.

Fortitude

We must stand strong and be brave when we face difficulties and challenges in our lives. God will give us the strength and power to withstand all circumstances, no matter how difficult they may seem. He wants us to remember that love is the key to smoothing over hard times, and we will remain calm, strong, and in control, with Him at our side.

January 12

James 5:10-11

Brothers and sisters, as an example of patience in the face of suffering, take the prophets who spoke in the name of the Lord. As you know, we count as blessed those who have persevered. You have heard of Job's perseverance and have seen what the Lord finally brought about. The Lord is full of compassion and mercy.

Protection

Good things come to those that wait, so we wait on the Lord and look for His goodness. His love pierces through the darkness, and rescues us from our suffering. We persevere knowing God is with us, and lovingly blesses us with all that is good.

January 13

Hebrews 11:1-2

Now faith is being sure of what we hope for and certain of what we do not see.

Faith

We must trust in the Lord completely—everything is under His control. He can move mountains and take all of our difficulties away, but there is so much to learn in waiting. For out of waiting comes perseverance, hope, faith, trust and self-control. We wait on the Lord, for He is good, his love endures forever.

January 14

2 Timothy 2:11-13

This is a faithful saying:

For if we died with Him,

We shall also live with Him

If we endure,

We shall also reign with Him

If we deny Him,

He will also deny us.

If we are faithless,

He remains faithful;

He cannot deny himself.

Faith

There may be times we do not follow the path God leads us on, and times we may turn our back on God all together. But even in those trying times, God will not turn His back on us. If we have lost our way, He promises to show us the way back. He loves us that much; His love never fails.

January 15

1 Timothy 6:6-10

But godliness with contentment is great gain. For we brought nothing into this world, and we can take nothing out of it. But if we have food and clothing, we can be content with that. People who want to get rich fall into temptation and a trap and into many foolish and harmful desires that plunge men into ruin and destruction.

For the love of money is a root of all evil. Some people, eager for money, have wandered from the faith and pierced themselves with many griefs.

Humility

Often, we look around and fall into the trap of seeing all that we don't have, instead of being happy and feeling blessed with all that we do. Follow God's direction and know that the riches of this world are not what God wants us to desire. He wants us to desire Him, plain and simple. God is where true happiness is found.

January 16

2 Corinthians 12:9-10

But he said to me, "My grace is sufficient for you, for my power is made perfect in weakness." Therefore I will boast the more gladly about my weaknesses, so that Christ's power may rest on me. That is why for Christ's sake, I delight in weaknesses, in insults, in hardships, in persecution, in difficulties. For when I am weak then I am strong.

Protection

Jesus's ability to come to our aid when we are powerless, weak, and disheartened is a true blessing. He comes to help us in our time of need, and we can feel his love, strength, and comfort. His power rests on us and becomes our power to go out and serve him in love and kindness.

January 17

Isaiah 40:31

Those that hope in the Lord will renew their strength. They will soar on wings like eagles; they will run and not grow weary, they will walk and not be faint.

Hope

When life is difficult and challenges surmount, know that you can rely on the Lord for your strength, that you can rely on the Lord for absolutely everything. He will give you what you need in the moment you need it, and in His love and goodness, He will come to your side.

January 18

Ephesians 3:12

Because of Christ and our faith in Him, we can now come fearlessly into God's presence, assured of His glad welcome.

Faith

It takes faith, strength, and confidence to show up and say to God, "Here I am Lord, do with me what you will." When you do, you will let go of your agenda and take on His. God's way is a much better one; it will lead to a life that is fruitful and full of His peace.

January 19

Matthew 6:6

If you want to pray, go into your room, shut the door, and pray to your Father in secret and your Father who sees in secret, will reward you.

Obedience

When you pray, go into your room—which could mean going into your inner self, where God dwells. Do not ask for anything, just sit with God in silence. He knows what you need before you even ask, and He delights in your friendship, your closeness, your love. He will give you your heart's desires if they are His will for you, so be still and revel in His love.

January 20

Matthew 11:28-30

Come to me, all you who labor and are burdened and I will give you rest. Take my yoke upon you and learn from me, for I am meek and humble of heart, and you will find rest for yourselves. For my yoke is easy, and my burden light.

Guidance

God wants us to come to Him; to drop our cares, our fears, our load, and give it to Him. God will take it all and make our way a little lighter. He is our comforter and in Him we find true rest.

January 21

2 Chronicles 15:2

The Lord is with you when you are with him. If you seek him, he will be found by you.

Knowledge

To know God is to seek His presence and to align yourself with His thoughts, wishes, and future for you. If you earnestly want to know Him, then reach out to Him in prayer. God wants to be in your life, and welcomes your seeking Him with His love.

January 22

Psalm 32:8

I will instruct you and teach you in the way you should go. I will counsel you and watch over you.

Guidance

God's guidance is wonderful; keep an open heart and a listening ear to the Holy Spirit living in us and with us. We are guided, taught, and watched over, all at the same time. When God's desires and our desires are one, that is what leads to true happiness.

January 23

Jeremiah 24:7

I will give them a heart to know me, that I am Lord. They will be my people, and I will be their God, for they will return to me with all their heart.

Knowledge

God knows you. He loves you and He created you. If you stray, He is there. If you forget about Him, He is there. If you never knew Him, get to know Him now, it is not too late. For He is our God and we are His people, and He loves you.

January 24

James 4:8

Come near to God and He will come near to you.

Guidance

The closer you come to God, the closer He will come to you. He will show you all your heart's desires, wishes, and longings, and lead you on the right path to fulfilling them. All these things He has placed in your heart from the beginning, and wants to see them carried out as much as you do.

January 25

Luke 9:23-25

If anyone would come after me, he must deny himself and take up his cross daily and follow me. For whoever wants to save his life, will lose it, but whoever loses his life for me will save it. What good is it for a man to gain the whole world, yet lose or forfeit his very self.

Obedience

God desires that we obey Him and His plans for us. Sometimes, that means going against what we think is right for us, and doing what God thinks is right. He has a plan and He knows what is good.

January 26

Matthew 5:14-16

You are the light of the world. A city on the hill cannot be hidden. Neither do people light a lamp and put it under a bowl. Instead they put it on a stand and it gives light to everyone in the house. In the same way, let your light shine before men so they may see your good deeds and praise your Father in Heaven.

Joy

The joy from knowing God and walking in His light and love, is what God wants us to spread to the whole world. When we are this light and beauty, we shine in everything we do. We will then attract others to Him, and further His Kingdom on earth, a true gift and blessing.

January 27

Hebrews 12:10

They disciplined us for a little while as they thought best; but God disciplines us for our good, that we may share in his holiness.

Guidance

God disciplines us so that we can learn, grow, and find our strength; and in fortitude and love, do the work He intends us to do. He guides us and shows us the way if we listen. His work is the way we share His holiness and goodness on this earth with others.

January 28

Proverbs 4:23

Above all else, guard your heart, for it is the wellspring of life.

Love

Our heart is an instrument for carrying God's love, so keep it open, pure, and fine-tuned. If someone offends you, guard your heart and make sure you do not allow that to seep in. God wants us to be joyous and happy so we can lead abundant and fulfilling lives.

January 29

Psalm 46:10

Be still and know that I am God.

Knowledge

In the hustle and bustle of everyday life, know God is present, God is love, and God is guiding you throughout your day. Be still and listen, and in those quiet moments, He touches your soul and will reveal His inmost desires for you.

January 30

Acts 15:9

He purified their hearts by faith.

Faith

Life can be challenging at times, and as we face those challenges, we go back to our faith—faith in a God we do not see, but feel deep down in our soul. In each difficulty we encounter that God sees us through, our heart is not only purified and cleansed, but is stronger and more resilient to face anything else that comes our way.

January 31

Galatians 5:16-18

So I say live by the Spirit, and you will not gratify the desires of the sinful nature. For the sinful nature desires what is contrary to the Spirit and Spirit what is contrary to the sinful nature.

They are in conflict with each other, so that you do not do what you want. But if you are led by the Spirit, you are not under the law.

Obedience

When we are living a life of sin and succumb to earthly desires—lust, greed, fame, material possessions—we are not living a life in the Spirit. The Spirit and its desires bring us true peace and contentment. The sinful nature can never bring us true happiness, but the Spirit and all its fruits—love, joy, peace, patience, kindness, goodness, faithfulness, gentleness, and self-control—will.

February 1

1 Corinthians 10:13

And God is faithful, he will not let you be tempted beyond what you can bear, but when you are tempted he will provide a way out so that you can stand up to it.

Protection

There will be temptations that come our way and some of them may be hard to bear. Remember that God will show you the way to overcome them. Look to Him, pray to Him, even cry out to Him. He loves you and wants to help you in your time of need.

February 2

Isaiah 50:4

He wakens me morning by morning, wakens my ear to listen like one being taught.

Guidance

God wants to be our guiding force from morning to night, but we need to listen. He is there in the gentle whispers that touch our souls. Listen to Him and open your heart.

February 3

Psalm 51:1-2

Have mercy on me, O God according to your unfailing love; according to your great compassion blot out my transgressions. Wash away all my iniquity and cleanse me from my sin.

Love

When we feel we are not all that we can be for God, when we have failed or come up short, come close to God. His love and mercy will never fail us. Draw near, so near to Him, that we can feel ourselves cleansed and made whole once again. His love can restore and renew us, always.

February 4

John 8:12

I am the light of the world. Whoever follows me will never have darkness, but will have the light of life.

Hope

When you walk with God and follow His ways, you let go of darkness—fear, anger, doubt, insecurity, and sadness—and instead exemplify the light—hope, happiness, purity, confidence, and love. The light always pierces through the darkness, so go forward and let your light shine bright for all the world to see.

February 5

Mark 11:24

Therefore I tell you, whatever you ask in prayer, believe that you will receive it, and it will be yours.

Faith

God wants you to ask for your heart's desires—you must believe and trust that if God wants those desires for you, He will freely give them. Have faith and expect good things, and good things will happen. God is a loving God, and He always wants the best for you.

February 6

Matthew 9: 9-13

I did not come to call the righteous but the sinner.

Obedience

Come to God with all your shortcomings, sins, and failures. It is exactly where you need to be: close to Him. Strive to be a better person every day. Set a daily intention and follow it. As long as it comes from a pure heart, and is purposeful, God will help you achieve it.

February 7

Matthew 9:37

The harvest is plentiful but the workers are few.

Obedience

We need God, but He needs us, too. He needs our hands to reach out and serve others, which can be as simple as giving someone a warm embrace. He needs our feet to go to the places no one else will go and do the work that is not always glamorous or makes us rich. He needs our hearts to give love abundantly to those who need a smile or a hand to hold in time of need. God's work is not always easy, but comes with bountiful rewards.

February 8

Psalm 138: 1-3

I will worship at your holy temple, and give thanks to your name.

Because of your kindness and your truth; for you have made great above all things your name and your promise. When I called, you answered me;

You built up strength within me.

Fortitude

When you are faced with challenges and lose your strength, call upon the Lord. He hears your prayers and will answer you in your pain and weakness. He will give you the strength and courage needed to see you through.

February 9

Philippians 4:6-7

Do not be anxious about anything, but in everything by prayer and petition, with thanksgiving, present your requests to God. And the peace of God, which transcends all understanding, will guard your hearts and minds in Jesus.

Trust

God wants to give you all that is good. Come to Him in prayer and thank Him ahead of time for all that He is going to do for you. Placing your trust in Him will give you a sense of peace and security, knowing that He not only listens, but he cares.

February 10

Psalm 23: 1-6

The Lord is my shepherd, I shall not be in want. He makes me lie down in green pastures, he leads me besides quiet waters, he restores my soul. He guides me in paths righteousness for his name's sake. Even though I walk through the valley of death I will fear no evil for you are with me. You prepare a table before me in the presence of my enemies. You anoint my head with oil, my cup overflows. Surely goodness and love will follow me all the days of my life and I will dwell in the house of the Lord forever.

Love

God will restore and heal us when walk with Him and live in Him. He wants us to come to Him and find true rest. We will be lacking in nothing with the Lord on our side; love and goodness will surround us all the days of our lives.

February 11

Luke 11:9-10

Ask and it will be given to you; seek and you will find; knock and the door will be opened to you. For everyone who asks receives; he seeks finds; and to him who knocks the door will be open

Hope

When you need something in your life that is important to you, just ask—but after you ask, seek to see what it is God truly wants for you. The door will be opened; He will either give you what your heart desires or lead you on a different path to getting what you want. Either way, trust that it will be good, because it is coming from the Lord.

February 12

Luke 18:7-8

And will not God bring about justice for His chosen ones who cry out to Him day and night? Will He keep putting them off? I tell you, He will see that they get justice and get it quickly.

Fortitude

God hears our pleas and our prayers. He will make sure justice is served when we call to Him, because He truly does want to right what is wrong. However, we need to be patient, because God's timing is not always ours.

February 13

Matthew 8:8

Lord, I do not deserve to have you come under my roof. But just say the word, and my servant will be healed.

Humility

When we ask the Lord to come into our lives, to heal us or be near, do so humbly. We open our eyes and recognize that this God of ours is an awesome God who can do more for us than we can imagine. So be humble before Him, and He will listen and answer your prayers.

February 14

Matthew 4: 19-20

Come follow me Jesus said and I will make you fishers of men. At once they left their nets and followed him.

Obedience

When you hear God's voice telling you to do something, whether big or small, listen to His calling. He has the perfect plans for you, so follow Him; willingly, prayerfully, and with determination and wonderful things will unfold.

February 15

Proverbs 16:9

In their hearts humans plan their course, but the Lord establishes their steps.

Guidance

As humans we want to plan our lives and have things under control and that is fine to a point, but God is the one who should be our lead. God is our guide, God is our foundation, and God lays the groundwork. He wants to lead us on the way we should go, and with humility and grace we can follow.

February 16

Romans 8:38-39

For I am convinced that neither death nor life, neither angels or demons, neither present or future, nor any powers, neither height nor depth, not anything else in all creation, will be able to separate us from the love of God that is in Christ Jesus.

Protection

In our highest of highs or lowest of lows, in our doubts, our fears, or overwhelming obstacles, absolutely nothing will separate us from His love. Be certain of this love in your heart, and be thankful of God's closeness to you, for it is the greatest of gifts.

February 17

Psalm 112

Praise the Lord

Blessed are those that fear the Lord,

Who find great delight in his commands.

Their children will be might in the land;

The generation of the upright will be blessed.

Wealth and riches are in their houses,

And their righteousness endures forever.

Even in darkness light dawns for the upright,

For those who are gracious and compassionate and righteous,

Good will come to those who are generous and lend freely,

Who conduct their affairs with justice.

Surely the righteous will never be shaken;

They will be remembered forever.

They will have no fear of bad news;

Their hearts are steadfast and trusting in the Lord.

Their hearts are secure, they will have no fear;

In the end they will look in triumph on their foes.

They have freely scattered their gifts to the poor,

Their righteousness endures forever; their horn will be lifted up in honor.

Fortitude

A person who lives for the Lord is strong in the Lord's love, and is secure in his path forward. He does not fear the future when hard times come, because he places everything in God's hands and says, "let your will be done," and all is well.

February 18

Matthew 18:19-20

Again I tell you that if two of you on earth agree about anything you ask for; it will be done for you by my Father in heaven. For where two or three come together in my name, there I am with them.

Obedience

When we come together with one another in prayer, and we pray for God's will to be done in both the big and the small things in life, He is there in our midst. God wants to bless us abundantly and give us all that is good. Pray for his blessings and be thankful for all that you will receive.

February 19

Psalm 87: 7

As they make music they will sing "My home is within you."

Joy

Accept God into your heart, into your entire being, and know that He wants to make His home in you. Make it a place He will feel welcome, make it a place He would want to dwell. Free from worry and care, filled with God's joy, let Him come and make His home in you, and you will feel safe and secure knowing He is there.

February 20

John 17:3-4

Now this is eternal life; that they may know you, the only true God, and Jesus Christ whom you have sent. I have brought you glory on Earth by completing the work you gave me to do.

Obedience

God has plans for each and every one of us. If we are prompted by His nudges, quiet whispers, and gentle guidance, we will be on the right path to completing what He put us on the earth to do. We will do it all with His strength and peace, holding us steady, and leading us forward every step of the way.

February 21

John 17:17

Sanctify them by the truth, your word is truth.

Knowledge

God sanctifies us and sets us apart by what we believe. If we believe in Him and His teachings, He will bring us into His glory. His word is truth, His word is freedom, and His word is peace.

February 22

Mark 9:23

"Everything is possible for one who believes." Immediately the boy's father exclaimed. "I do believe; help me overcome my unbelief."

Faith

Jesus tells us that "everything is possible for one who believes," and we want to believe, yet sometimes it is difficult. We want to believe we can climb the highest mountain and cross the widest river and keep running and not stumble and fall. So how do we do so? Ask Jesus to help remove those fears, doubts, and obstacles, and he will.

February 23

Mark 9:37

Whoever welcomes one of these little children in my name welcomes me; and whoever welcomes me does not welcome me but the one who sent me.

Humility

We are all children of God. When you welcome a child or a person who is new in their faith to Jesus, it is a beautiful act of love and kindness. Jesus wants us to know that it is ultimately himself you are welcoming into that person's life through your act of kindness, and all are welcome in God's Kingdom.

February 24

Mark 10: 29-31

"Truly I tell you," Jesus replied, "no one has left home or brothers or sisters or mother or father or children or fields for me and the gospel will fail to receive a hundred times as much in this present age: homes, brothers, sisters, mothers, children and fields—along with persecutions—and in the age to come eternal life. But many who are first will be last and the last first.

Humility

We oftentimes want to be the ones who are the most knowledgeable, or people that have the highest class or stature. Jesus says, *I need you to not put your faith in possessions, or things that keep you from knowing me intimately, but desire all that I want for you.* Jesus looks at the ones who are humble as the greatest, and the ones who are full of pride as the least of ones.

February 25

Luke 1:45

Blessed is she that believed that what the Lord has said to her will be accomplished.

Faith

Mary believed that God would and could do the unfathomable; that through her, a virgin, the Son of God would be born. If we have the faith Mary had, even a tiny fraction of it, we truly will have a trusting heart and do the things God intends of us on this earth.

February 26

Psalm 100:5

For the Lord is good and his love endures forever; his faithfulness continues through all generations.

Faith

God is faithful to us for all time. From generation to generation His word, His love, His guidance is lasting. We are blessed that we can always turn to Him. His love is endless and endures forever.

February 27

2 Peter 3:14-15

So dear friends, since you are looking forward to this, make every effort to be found spotless, blameless and at peace with him. Bear in mind that our Lord's patience means salvation, just as our dear brother Paul also wrote you with the wisdom that God gave him.

Obedience

God wants others to see the God in us. When we are an example of love, honesty, and peace, and all the other amazing qualities God bestows upon us, then others can see we have been touched by God. They see something in us that they want, and in seeing they can start believing God can be in their lives too.

February 28

Psalm 62:5

Find rest, oh my soul, in God alone; my hope comes from him.

Peace

The rest for your soul that comes from knowing, praying, and living with God, is rest like no other. Our soul is satisfied when it rests in Him. We feel a peace and understanding that can only come from God, our Creator. When we find Him, we find a place our soul can not only rest, but be at home.

March 1

Matthew 13: 45-46

Again the kingdom of heaven is like a merchant looking for fine pearls. When he found one of great value, he sold everything he had and bought it.

Knowledge

We know the kingdom of heaven is precious and is of great value. Everything we do on earth is to attain it, and where is the kingdom of heaven? The kingdom of heaven is both in God's heavenly realms and here on earth. Make your life one of loving, serving, and graciously living a life of God's will for you, and you will spread God's kingdom here on earth.

March 2

Matthew 15: 25-28

The woman came and knelt before him. "Lord, help me!" she said.

He replied, "It is not right to take the children's bread and toss it to the dogs."

"Yes it is Lord", she said. "Even the dogs eat the crumbs that fall from their master's table."

Then Jesus said to her, "Woman you have great faith! Your request is granted." And her daughter was healed at that moment.

Faith

When we cry out to Jesus, especially in our most trying times, he hears us. He sees our faith and he will heal us, or move obstacles out of our way. And in our belief that he can do anything, he comes to our side and says "Here I am."

March 3

Matthew 16:19

I will give you the keys to the kingdom of heaven; whatever you bind on earth will be bound in heaven and whatever you loose on earth will be loosed in heaven.

Obedience

Whatever we hold tight to, whatever we treasure on this earth, is what we will treasure in heaven, and whatever we let go of, we will release in heaven. Treasure the things that are everlasting: joy, peace, love, and kindness. Let go of the things that don't serve you: greed, worldly possessions, lust, and control. The keys to the kingdom are waiting and God wants you to be a part of His kingdom.

March 4

John 6:51

I am the living bread that came down from heaven. If anyone eats of this bread, he will live forever. This bread is my flesh, which I give for the life of the world.

Hope

Jesus sacrificed his body so that we will have him with us always, through his Spirit that lives in us. His flesh, this bread, sustains us, nourishes us and gives us life. We know if we live with him here on earth, we will live with him forever. He feeds us abundantly with his love.

March 5

Psalm 37:4

Delight yourself in the Lord and he will give you the desires of your heart.

Joy

Fill your heart with God's love, joy, and peace, and out of this, good things will come. He knows your heart's desires because He created you with those desires. He created you with a pure and hopeful heart. Keep loving, hoping, and trusting that all your desires will come true, and know that your God is a loving God who wants to bless you.

March 6

Psalm 91:1

He who dwells in the shelter of the Most High will rest in the shadow of the Almighty.

Protection

When we stay close to God, and dwell in His presence, we are sheltered, safe, and secure. He takes us into His care and we rest knowing all is well, and we are safe in His loving gaze and in His arms.

March 7

Matthew 5:3-12

Blessed are the poor in spirit,

For theirs is the kingdom of heaven

Blessed are those that mourn

For they will be comforted

Blessed are the meek,

For they will inherit the earth

Blessed are those who hunger and thirst for righteousness

For they will be filled

Blessed are the merciful,

For they will see God

Blessed are the peacemakers,

For they will be called sons of God

Blessed are those who are persecuted for righteousness,

For theirs is the kingdom of heaven

Love

We are blessed by God when we are called to follow Jesus's teachings. To follow Jesus in peace, mercy, and humility, and in all that he calls us to do on this earth, is a true blessing to us and to others. Follow

Jesus and open your heart to a life filled with joy, peace, love, and many blessings.

March 8

Zechariah 4:6

"Not by might nor by power but by my Spirit" says the Lord Almighty

Guidance

We sometimes think by forcing or coercing, or through our own strength, we will get what we want or what we think would be good for us—but God thinks differently. God says to go quietly, gently, at ease, with His Spirit, and you will get what you want if it is His will for you. Approach the matter in this way and God will show you what is best for you and for others.

March 9

1 John 4:7-9

Dear Friends, let us love one another for love comes from God. Everyone who loves has been born of God. Whoever does not love does not know God, because God is love. This is how God showered His love among us. He sent his one and only son into the world that we might live through him.

Love

If we are born of God and have God in us, we need to love all. God's way is loving the people who challenge us, as well as the people who adore us and love us immensely. God's love in us sees the love in others. We know that God so loved the world that He sent His only Son so that his love lives in us, and we will live through him.

March 10

Deuteronomy 33:27

The eternal God is your refuge, and underneath are the everlasting arms.

Protection

God is our strength, our comforter, and our protector. He is in us, besides us, and underneath us, holding us when we need His strength and fortitude, but also when we need rest. Look to the Lord for refuge, a safe haven, and protection from anything that might come our way.

March 11

Luke 9:11

He welcomed them and spoke to them about the kingdom of God, and healed those who needed healing.

Love

Jesus healed those that came to him, and he wants to come to us today and heal us from all our afflictions. Whether it be spiritual, emotional or physical healing, he wants us to ask for his healing touch. He loves us and can restore us to a healthy, thriving, and loving existence.

March 12

Isiah 30:15

By waiting and by calm you shall be saved, in quiet and in trust your strength lies.

Guidance

In our impatience to bring about change in our lives or take control, God tells us to wait. Wait and be calm, He will show us the way to go—step by step. Listen to His guidance, listen to His promptings, know that you can trust Him, gain your strength from it all, and wait.

March 13

Ephesians 3:17-18

And I pray that you being rooted in and established in love, may have power together with all the saints, to grasp how wide, long, high and deep the love of Christ is.

Love

Jesus's love knows no boundaries. His love is so deep and encompassing that we cannot help but feel its power. In times when you need to feel Christ's love, call out to him in prayer, and feel that abundant joy and peace wash over you when you do.

March 14

Psalm 119: 105

Your word is a lamp to my feet and a light to my path.

Guidance

When we cannot see the way and our path forward is not clear, we know that God is watching over us. He will guide us on the way to go if we look for His light in the darkness. His light and His words shine brightly and guide us so we do not fear, but instead go forward boldly in His love.

March 15

1 Peter 5: 10-11

And the God of all grace, who called you to his eternal glory in Christ, after you have suffered a little while, will himself restore you and make you strong, firm and steadfast. To him be the power forever and ever.

Fortitude

When we go through suffering in this life—and we all do at some point—we gain perseverance, fortitude, compassion and hope. We lean on God to get us through, and when we do, we will gain the strength and the knowledge to help others in their time of need: a true gift from God.

March 16

Matthew 7:6

Do not give dogs what is sacred; do not throw your pearls to pigs. If you do they may trample them under their feet, and then turn and tear them to pieces.

Protection

There may be people in your life who challenge you, or do not find sacred what you find sacred. Do not let them rob you of your peace. Instead, turn to God, the great protector of your mind, body, and soul, and let Him fill you with His love, peace, and understanding. Follow His path and His ways, and you will be blessed.

March 17

Mark 4:1-9, 13-20

Listen! A farmer went out to sow his seed. As he was scattering the seed some fell along the path, and the birds came and ate it up. Some fell on rocky places, where it did not have much soil. It sprang up quickly, because the soil was shallow. But when the sun came up, the plants were scorched, and they withered because they had no root. Other seeds fell upon the thorns, which grew up and choked the plants, so they did not bear grain. Still others fell on the good soil. It came up, grew and produced a crop, multiplying thirty, sixty or even a hundred times. Then Jesus said he who has ears let him hear. Then Jesus said to them, "Don't you understand this parable. The farmer sows the word. Some people are like seeds along the path where the word is sown. As soon as they hear it, Satan comes takes away that which was sown in them. Others are like seed sown on rocky places, hear the word and at once receive it with joy. But since they have no root, they only last a short time. When trouble or persecution comes because of the word, they quickly fall away. Still others, are like seed sown among the thorns hear the word; but the worries of this life the deceitfulness of wealth and the desires for other things come in and choke the word, making it unfruitful. Other like seeds sown on good soil, hear the word, accept it, and produce a crop, thirty, sixty, or even a hundred times what was sown.

Obedience

God wants to plant His seed, His word, in us. Is the soil, our hearts, ready and rich and are we open to receive the seed? When we are ready, this seed can produce much fruit and we will bring others to Him, and blossom into all that He desires for us. And the fruit will multiply.

March 18

Luke 9:48

Whoever welcomes this little child in my name welcomes me; and whoever welcomes me welcomes the one who sent me. For he who is least among you all, is the greatest.

Humility

Jesus wants us to walk through this life as little children: humble, kind, meek, full of trust and love. He loves us and doesn't need us to prove anything to him, or make something of ourselves that we are not. We who are least among people are the greatest in his eyes.

March 19

John 15: 12-17

Love each other as I have loved you. Greater love has no one than this, that he lay down his life for his friends. You are my friends if you do what I command. I no longer call you servants, because a servant does not know his master's business, for everything I learned from my Father, I have made known to you. You did not choose me but I chose you and appointed you to go bear fruit—fruit that will last. Then the Father will give you whatever you ask in my name. This is my command: Love each other.

Love

Jesus has work for us to do, and it all starts with love. Love in our hearts, love for others, love for ourselves. We are his chosen ones, and we are chosen to love.

March 20

Luke 13:18-19

What is the kingdom of God like? It is like a mustard seed which man took and planted in the garden. It grew and became a tree, and the birds of the air perched in its branches.

Love

The tiniest of seeds, a mustard seed can grow into the largest of plants, that the birds can perch in and feel safe and supported. Our faith can start out very small at first, but like the mustard seed, can grow into a great faith. Then others can come as we spread our arms, the branches, out in love. Let our faith grow big for others to see and draw near to us in God's love.

March 21

John 15:5-8

I am the vine you are the branches. If a man remains in me and I in him, he will bear fruit; apart from me you can do nothing. If anyone does not remain in me, he is like a branch that is thrown away and withers, such branches are picked up and thrown into the fire. If you remain in me and I in you, ask whatever you wish and it will be given you. This is to my Father's glory, that you bear fruit, showing yourselves to be my disciples.

Obedience

If we are to do Jesus's work here on earth, we must remain in him. Be loving, prayerful, kind, and listen to all that he wants from you. Ask anything in Jesus's name, for his sake and glory, and he will grant it. Jesus wants to spread goodness in this world, and needs us as much as we need him to do so.

March 22

John 8:12

I am the light of the world. Whoever follows me will never walk in darkness, but will have the light of life.

Joy

Jesus wants to illuminate us, both inside and out. When we walk in his light, and follow his paths, we see things as they truly are. The darkness will fade away and all that is left is a light that guides us, and fills our hearts with a radiance and joy.

March 23

Matthew 18:21-22

Then Peter said to Jesus and asked, "Lord how many times shall I forgive my brother or sister who sins against me? Up to seven times?" Jesus answered, "I tell you, not seven times, but seventy-seven times."

Humility

Forgiving others is something we are called to do, even in the most trying of times. Jesus's life was all about forgiveness, and he taught us there is no limit to how many times we are to forgive others. It will ultimately lead to peace and healing, for others as well as for ourselves.

March 24

2 Corinthians 3:17-18

Now the Lord is the Spirit, and where the Spirit of the Lord is, there is freedom. And we all, who with unveiled faces contemplate the Lord's glory, are being transformed into his image with ever increasing glory, which comes from the Lord, who is the Spirit.

Joy

We are one with Jesus as the Spirit enters into our lives. We shed the layers of our false selves to come into our true selves. When we embody all that Jesus is—love, peace, joy, goodness—it is evident to all.

March 25

Psalm 34:1-3

I will extol the Lord at all times, his praise will always be on my lips. Glorify the Lord with me; let us exalt his name together.

Joy

Praise God at all times, both in the good times and when we are facing challenges. When we praise and thank God, we open a channel and He listens. He hears our words of praise, and He helps us in our time of need, and celebrates too in our most joyous of times.

March 26

Luke 24:32

They asked each other "Were our hearts not burning within us while he talked with us on the road and opened the scripture to us?

Knowledge

When Jesus speaks to us, let us open our ears to what he tells us—but more importantly, let us open our hearts to what he desires of us. It is our hearts that lead us to do Jesus's work here on earth and we know that if it is his desire, it will be fulfilled.

March 27

John 4:11-16

Dear Friends, since God so loved us, we also ought to love one another. No one has ever seen God; but if we love one another, God lives in us and his love is made complete in us.

This is how we know that we live in him and he in us; He has given us his Spirit. And we have seen and testify that the Father has sent his Son to be the Savior of the world. If anyone acknowledges that Jesus is the Son of God, God lives in them and they in God. And so we know and rely on the love God has for us.

God is love. Whoever lives in love lives in God, and God in them.

Love

Love is in us when God is in us, and God lives in us through His Spirit. If we ask God to make His home in us, it is easy to love one another. Our love will abound for all mankind.

March 28

John 3:5-8

Jesus answered, "Very truly I tell you, no one can enter the kingdom of God unless they are born of the Spirit. Flesh gives birth to flesh, but Spirit gives birth to Spirit. You should not be surprised at my saying, you must be born again. The wind blows wherever it pleases. You hear its sound, but you cannot tell where it comes from or where it is going. So it is with everyone born of the Spirit.

Guidance

If we are born of the Spirit, we give up our earthly ways and follow Jesus into a new life. A life of love, a life of purity of mind and heart, a life that is born of a new nature. We put our old ways behind us and we walk in his light and his love. We are born anew.

March 29

John 14:12-14

Very truly I tell you, whoever believes in me will do the works I have been doing, and they will do even greater things than these, because I am going to the Father. And I will do whatever you ask in my name, so that the Father will be glorified in the Son. You may ask for anything in my name and I will do it.

Faith

We are called to do great things for God, and will do even greater things than we can imagine because Jesus blesses us and is one with the Father. We can ask Jesus for anything and if it be his will for us, he will grant it. We ask and then we place it in his hands, and we trust that whatever the outcome, it will ultimately be the right one.

March 30

John 6:35

I am the light of life. Whoever comes to me will never go hungry, and whoever believes in me will never be thirsty.

Faith

Jesus fulfills all our needs even when we don't see it. He is our sustenance, the bread of life. He fills all our needs and we will never want. Be satisfied with the food he provides through his body which he sacrificed, and the water which is his Spirit, which is overflowing.

March 31

Matthew 1:23

The Virgin will be with child and give birth to a son, and they will call him Immanuel which means "God with us."

Peace

The Virgin Mary was delivered a message from God that she would bear a child and call him Jesus, and as a result she put all her fears, doubts, and wonder aside and said "Yes" to God. When God calls on us to do something that we question, or something we do not know how to accomplish, are we able to say "Yes," too? God will work out the details—just listen to His voice and guidance, and trust in His plans.

April 1

Colossians 3: 12-14

Therefore, as God's chosen people, holy and dearly loved, clothe yourselves with compassion, kindness, humility, gentleness and patience. Bear with each other and forgive whatever grievances you may have against another. Forgive, as the Lord forgave you. And over all these virtues put on love, which binds them all together in perfect unity.

Love

Showing compassion to others can sometimes be difficult. There are people, situations, and times in our lives that can challenge us. As people of God, clothe yourself in compassion, kindness, humility, gentleness, and patience. Over all, cloak yourself in love, which brings everything together, and know that love is the ultimate blessing from God.

April 2

John 10:27-30

My sheep listen to my voice; I know them, and they follow me. I give them eternal life, and they shall never perish; no one can snatch them out of my hand. My Father who has given them to me, is greater than all; no one can snatch them out of my Father's hand. I and the Father are one.

Protection

Jesus is our shepherd. He guides us, loves us, and most of all, protects us. No one can take us away from his love, or that of our Father in heaven. We hear his voice and we follow him faithfully.

April 3

Psalm 68:5

A father to the fatherless, a defender of widows is God in his holy dwelling.

Protection

God is the protector and champion of the fatherless, widows, and all those who are poor and afflicted. His heart overflows to those that need His healing touch and affection. God is a loving God, that comes to those in need, and His love will never fail us.

April 4

John 15:9-11

As the Father has loved me so I loved you. Now remain in my love. If you keep my commands you will remain in my love, just as I have kept my Father's commands and remain in his love. I have told you this so that my joy may be in you and your joy complete.

Love

Jesus wants to give us his unfailing love. He also wants us to love others as he loved us. This takes a big heart, but can bring us amazing joy. We are to be love in this world, and we can do this because we are loved by him.

April 5

John 12: 44-46

Then Jesus cried out, "Whoever believes in me does not believe only in me, but the one who sent me. The one who looks at me is seeing the one who sent me. I have come into the world as a light, so that no one who believes in me should stay in darkness.

Joy

Jesus gives us light, and delivers us from any darkness we might have in our lives. He also gave us this light so that we can share it with others. The world can, at times, be a dark and lonely place, but not if we shed Jesus's light to others with a smile, sound advice, good deeds, or by having a positive attitude. We can be light, peace, love, and joy in this world, and in turn, make it a better place.

April 6

James 1:2-6

Consider it pure joy, my brothers and sisters, whenever you face trials of many kinds, because you know that the testing of your faith produces perseverance. Let perseverance finish its work so that you may be mature and complete, not lacking anything. If any of you lacks wisdom, you should ask God, who gives generously to all without finding fault, and it will be given you. But when you ask, you must believe and not doubt, because the one who doubts is like a wave of the sea, blown and tossed by the wind.

Faith

Faith is something that grows in us continually. Trials may come that may cause us to turn to God. That is how we grow—when we depend on the Lord to get us through our trials. Persevering through our suffering and our doubts will lead us closer to God. When we trust and lean on Him, He will show us the way.

April 7

John 14:27

Peace I leave with you; my peace I give you. I do not give to you as the world gives. Do not let your hearts be troubled and do not be afraid.

Peace

Jesus is the one who can give us true peace. The world and all that it offers cannot. True peace comes from opening ourselves up to Jesus's love and his words. Amazing joy will come if we open our hearts, minds, and souls to God, Jesus and the Holy Spirit.

April 8

Philippians 2:1-5

Therefore if you have any encouragement from being united with Christ, if any comfort from his love, if any common sharing in the Spirit, if any tenderness and compassion, then make my joy complete by being like-minded, having the same love, being one in spirit and of one word. Do nothing out of selfish ambition or vain conceit. Rather in humility value others above yourselves, not looking to your own interests but each of you to the interests of others.

Humility

To put others first and look after their interests before your own, is the humble way to go about life. If we are to walk on this earth like Jesus, with humility, love, and compassion towards others, we will come with an open heart for the people that God puts into our lives.

April 9

Matthew 6:25-34

Therefore I tell you do not worry about your life, what you will eat or what you will drink, or about your body, what you will wear. Is not life more important than food, and the body more important than clothes? Look at the birds of the air, they do not sow or reap or store away in barns, and yet your heavenly Father feeds them. Who of your by worrying can add a single hour to your life?

And why do you worry about clothes? See how the lilies of the field grow. They do not labor or spin. Yet I tell you that not even Solomon in all his splendor was dressed like one of these. Is that how God clothes the grass of the field, which is here today and tomorrow is thrown into the fire, will he not much more clothe you, oh you of little faith? So do not worry saying, "What shall we eat?" or "what shall we wear?" For the pagans ran after all these things, and your heavenly Father knows that you need them. But seek first his Kingdom and his righteousness, and all these things will be given to you as well. Therefore do not worry about tomorrow for tomorrow will worry about itself, each day has enough trouble of its own.

Guidance

God knows what you need before you even ask Him. He does not want you to worry, but pray often for what you want. Prayers are the answer, not worry; talk to

God, listen to God, and He will give you the answers. Replace fear, anxiety, and worry, for love, joy, and peace, and your life will be better for it.

April 10

Psalm 139:7-10

Where can I go from your Spirit? Where can I flee from your presence? If I go to the heavens, you are there; if I make my bed in the depths you are there.

If I rise on the wings of the dawn, if I settle on the far side of the sea, even there your hand will guide me. Your right hand will hold me fast.

Protection

God is always there to protect and love us wherever we are in life. In our highs or lows, in our wandering or nearness to Him, He guides us and meets us exactly where we are. There is no way to escape His love. Let Him in your life and let Him hold you close. He loves you and wants to feel your love, too.

April 11

John 8:31-32

To the Jews who had believed him, Jesus said, "If you hold to my teaching, you are really my disciples. Then you will know the truth and the truth will set you free.

Knowledge

The words of Jesus can live in you, and when you know and understand them, it can open up a whole new world to you. The truth—His truth—will set you free, which means freedom from worry, freedom from care, and freedom from anything that keeps you from God.

April 12

Mark 4:24-25

Consider carefully what you hear. With the measure you use it will be measured to you and even more. Whoever has will be given more and whoever does not have, even what he has will be taken away.

Obedience

When we use our God-given talents, we will be blessed many times over. If we do not use the gifts that God has graciously given us, we are not living to our full potential. God created us for a purpose, and whatever we are destined to do on this earth should be sought after and will be fulfilled by Him.

April 13

1 Corinthians 13:1-13

If I speak in the tongues of men and of angels, but have not love I am only a resounding gong or a clanging cymbal. If I have the gift of prophesy and can fathom all mysteries and all knowledge, and if I have a faith that can move mountains, but have not love, I am nothing. If I give all I possess to the poor and surrender my body to the flames but have not love I gain nothing.

Love is patient, and love is kind. It does not envy, it does not boast, it is not proud. It is not rude, it is not self-seeking, it is not easily angered, if keeps no records of wrongs. Love does not delight in evil but rejoices with the truth. It always protects, always trusts, always hopes, always perseveres.

Love never fails. But where there are prophesies, they will cease; where there are tongues, they will be stilled; where there is knowledge it will pass away. For we know in part and we prophesy in part, but when perfection comes, the imperfect disappears. When I was a child, I reasoned like a child. When I became a man, I put childish ways behind me. Now we see but a poor reflection as in a mirror; then we shall see face to face. Now I know in part; then I shall know fully, even as I am fully known.

And now these three remain; faith, hope and love. But the greatest of these is love.

Love

Love is many things, and if it resides in our hearts at all times, it can be a powerful instrument for change. Love is selfless, love is kind, and love is pure. Love in our hearts is a gift to share. There is nothing more powerful than love.

April 14

2 Corinthians 1:3-4

Praise be to the God and the Father of our Lord Jesus Christ, the Father of compassion and the God of all comfort, who comforts us in all our troubles, so that we can comfort those in any trouble with the comfort we ourselves receive from God.

Hope

We turn to God when troubles seem too hard to bear and He is there to comfort and guide us. With the same compassion and comfort God gives us, we can in turn show love and comfort to those in need. God's love passes onto others, and hope is eternal.

April 15

Genesis 3:8-9

Then the man and his wife heard the sound of the Lord God as he was walking in the garden in the cool of the day, and they hid from the Lord God among the trees of the garden. But the Lord God called to the man, "Where are You?"

Obedience

God wants to know us. He wants to know where we are in our spiritual journey. Where are we in relation to Him? Where are we in relation to others? Where are we in relation to our own heart and soul? We need to ask of ourselves, "Where am I?" When He calls us, are we ready to say, "Here I am Lord."

April 16

Matthew 25:34-40

Then the King will say to those on the right, "Come, you who are blessed by my Father; take your inheritance, the kingdom prepared for you since the creation of the world. For I was hungry and you gave me something to eat, I was thirsty and you gave me drink. I was a stranger and you invited me in. I needed clothes and you clothed me. I was sick and you looked after me, I was in prison and you came to visit me. Then the righteous will answer him, "Lord when did we see you hungry and feed you, or thirsty and give you something to drink. When did we see you a stranger and invite you in, or needing clothes and clothe you? When did we see you sick or in prison and go to visit you?

The King will reply, Truly I tell you when you did for one of the least of my brothers and sisters of mine, you did for me.

Love

Giving to those in need takes a gracious and humble heart. There are so many people in need in this world. When we reach out to others and fill their needs, we are doing Christ's work here on earth. When we treat people with love, dignity, and respect, we are showing the love of Jesus to others.

April 17

John 21:19

Jesus said this to indicate the kind of death by which Peter would glorify God. Then he said to him, "Follow me!"

Obedience

Jesus says follow me and we must follow. Where do we follow him? Wherever he asks us to go. If we listen, he will tell us. If we have an open heart, he will guide us. If we trust deep down in our soul, he will lead us on the right path.

April 18

Isaiah 57:14

And it will be said:

"Build up, build up, prepare the road! Remove the obstacles out of the way of the people"

For this is what the high and exalted One says-

He who lives forever, whose name is holy: I live in a high place, but also with the one who is contrite and lowly in spirit, to revive the spirit of the lowly and to revive the heart of the contrite.

Guidance

When God wants something for you, He will guide you and remove the obstacles out of the way. Listen to His voice, letting Him guide you and love you along the way. He always wants the best for you, and sees and blesses your humble heart, and watches over you with His loving heart.

April 19

Matthew 6: 8-15

Do not be like them, for your Father in heaven knows what you need before you ask him.

This is then how you should pray:

"Our Father in heaven, hallowed be thy name, your kingdom come, your will be done, on earth as it is in heaven. Give us today our daily bread. And forgive us our debts, as we have forgiven our debtors. And lead us not into temptation, but deliver us from the evil one. For if you forgive other people when they sin against you, your heavenly Father will also forgive you. But if you do not forgive others their sins, your Father will not forgive your sins."

Guidance

Jesus tells us how we should pray. It is a simple prayer, but that does not mean it is always easy to follow. Follow God's lead every day and do not be tempted by all the things in life that can take you from Him. Most of all, forgive others as He forgave us. This daily prayer, given to us by Jesus, is the pillar of our faith.

April 20

Luke 9:13-17

He replied, "You give them something to eat." They answered, "We have only five loaves of bread and two fish – unless we go and buy food for all this crowd. (About five thousand were there.)

But he said to his disciples, "Have them sit down in groups of about 50 each, and everyone sat down. Taking the five loaves and two fish and looking up to heaven, he gave thanks and broke them. Then he gave them to the disciples to distribute to the people. They all ate and were satisfied, and the disciples picked up twelve basketfuls of broken pieces that were left over.

Hope

When we place our trust in God, He can do miracles. He not only wants to answer our prayers, He wants to give us all we ask for and more. He is a good and loving God; kind, gracious, and merciful, and from His love, blessings will overflow.

April 21

Romans 8:28-30

And we know that in all things God works for the good of those that love him, who have been called according to his purpose. For those God foreknew he also predestined to be conformed to the image of his Son, that he might be the firstborn among many brothers and sisters.

And those he predestined, he also called; those he called, he also justified; those he justified he also glorified.

Guidance

God wants us to do His will; He gives us a purpose in life and will work to help us achieve it. If we trust, we can do great things for Him. He calls us to do amazing things, and we will, in His strength, peace, and with His love.

April 22

John 7:37-39

On the last and greatest day of the festival, Jesus stood and said in a loud voice, "Let anyone who is thirsty come to me and drink. Whoever believes in me as scripture has said, rivers of living water will flow within them.

Joy

Jesus fills us with the Spirit, the Spirit that fills us to the brim with love, joy, and happiness—so much so, that it flows abundantly from our hearts to others. Let us receive Jesus fully into our hearts, so we can share his love.

April 23

1 Corinthians 16:13

Be on your guard; stand firm in the faith; be courageous; be strong. Do everything in love.

Obedience

God wants us to walk through this life strong and courageous, because He is right there besides us, walking with us. We must stand strong even when we don't feel strong, and most of all, stay close in His love and protection. Then we can go forward in confidence, spreading His love to others.

April 24

Psalm 27:13-14

I will remain confident in this:

I will see the goodness of the Lord in the land of the living.

Wait for the Lord;

Be strong and take heart

And wait for the Lord

Hope

God is there for us, even though sometimes we face challenges and do not feel His presence. That is when we need to remain in His love and wait—wait for what He has in store for you, knowing that He works everything according to His purpose, and His intentions are good.

April 25

Matthew 6:22

The eye is the lamp of the body. If your eyes are healthy; your whole body will be full of light.

Joy

There is a radiance that embodies you when you live with God, a radiance and a joy that penetrates your heart and soul and then shines from you for the whole world to see. We are to be the light of God's love, burning brightly for others.

April 26

Luke 10:38-42

Jesus entered a village where a woman whose name was Martha welcomed him. She had a sister named Mary who sat beside the Lord at his feet listening to him and said, "Lord do you not care that my sister has left me by myself to do the serving? Tell her to help me. The Lord said in reply, "Martha, Martha, you are anxious and worried about many things. There is need only of one thing. Mary has chosen the better part and it will not be taken from her."

Obedience

Mary is an example of how Christ wants you to love him. In simplicity, with an open heart, and in humility, she sat at Jesus's feet and loved him and was loved in return. In beauty and splendor, she soaked in his love; she had chosen the better way, and we are asked to do the same.

April 27

John 2:5

His mother said to the servants, "Do whatever he tells you."

Obedience

Just as Mary instructed the servants to do what Jesus told them to do, we need to listen to Jesus and do the same. As we listen to that small voice inside of us instructing us what to do, or which way to go, we too can be obedient to what Jesus is calling of us. Listen and you will be led down the right path.

April 28

Psalm 143:8

Let the morning bring me word of your unfailing love, for I have put my trust in you. Show me the way I should go, for to you I lift up my soul.

Trust

We look to the Lord in the morning, to guide our ways and lead us in the way we should go. All the while, we put our absolute trust in Him, knowing He will be with us throughout our day. Our souls, minds, and hearts connect, and we are one with God.

April 29

Proverbs 3:5-6

Trust in the Lord with all your heart, and lean not on your own understanding; in all your ways acknowledge him, and he will make your paths straight.

Trust

In our lives, we will encounter hardships and difficulties, and often we won't understand why they are happening. That is when we need to trust in God and lean into Him, and follow whatever road He is going to take us on. Surrender to Him, and know that His paths are safe, His plans are good, and His heart is big, and He will see you through to the end.

April 30

Psalm 40:4

Blessed is the one who trusts in the Lord.

Trust

In the big and the small things in life, trust in the Lord. When you trust in God for all things, you are able to live a more joyful life. A blessed and peaceful life it will be, when you trust in His goodness and in His love.

May 1

Acts 20:34-36

You yourselves know these hands of mine have supplied my own needs and the needs of my companions. In everything I did, I showed you by this kind of hard work we must help the weak, remembering the words the Lord Jesus himself said: it is more blessed to give than to receive.

Love

Giving of yourself, your time, talent and treasure, is a blessing to others but also to yourself. Giving when you expect nothing back in return, can be truly rewarding and lead to happiness. You may, or you may never know how your gift of giving helps someone, but if it comes from your heart, God rejoices in that.

May 2

Psalm 29:11

The Lord gives strength to his people; the Lord blesses his people with peace.

Peace

When you are feeling weak and you need God's strength, turn to God and feel His everlasting arms around you. Stop all that you are doing and be still, and feel His love and peace surround you. Gain your strength in knowing that God loves you unconditionally, and blesses the people who look to Him as their Lord.

May 3

John 14:23-24

Anyone who loves me will obey my teaching. My father will love them, and we will come to them and make our home with them.

Love

God loves us and dwells in us through the Holy Spirit. He lives in us as we live in Him. We share His love with others because He has blessed us to do so, and from the love we give, we get so much back in return.

May 4

Luke 6:37-38

Do not judge and you will not be judged. Do not condemn and you will not be condemned. Forgive and you will be forgiven. Give and it will be given to you. A good measure, pressed down, shaken together and running over, will be poured into your lap. For with the measure you use it will be measured to you.

Love

When we forgive others there comes healing, love, and peace. Forgiveness allows us to move forward. It gives our hearts a clean slate and releases us from our burdens. If the person you forgive does not forgive you, it is all right. Keep praying for that person and let God work things out in His holy way.

May 5

Galatians 5:13-14

You my brothers and sisters were called to be free. But do not use your freedom to indulge the flesh; rather serve one another humbly in love. For the entire law is fulfilled in keeping this one command. Love your neighbor as yourself.

Love

We must love and care for ourselves as well as the people around us: our family, our friends, and our neighbors. We are also called to be free from worry, free from care, and free to be ourselves in the unique way that God made us. When we are free to be God's creation and see the good around us, it is easy to love the people that God brings into our lives.

May 6

Luke 2:46-50

After three days they found him in the temple courts, sitting among the teachers, listening to them and asking them questions. Everyone who heard of him asked and was amazed at his understanding and his answers. When his parents saw him, they were astonished. "Son why have you treated us like this? Your father and I have been anxiously searching for you." "Why were you searching for me, he asked. Didn't you know I had to be in my Father's house."

Obedience

Jesus was naturally the most comfortable in the temple courts and his Father's house, because he was the Son of God. Whether you are at church or serving the Lord elsewhere, be comfortable with wherever God leads you or calls you to go. Listen to His guidance and be obedient in doing His will.

May 7

Mark 9:23-24

"Everything is possible for one who believes." Immediately the boy's father exclaimed, "I do believe; help me overcome my unbelief."

Faith

We are promised many great things from God if we believe. Even if we have a strong faith, it is natural to have moments that we doubt. We believe, yet when we waver ask for God's help. He will come to our side and strengthen us in our faith and help us to believe.

May 8

Lamentations 3:25-26, 28

The Lord is good to those who hope in him, to one who seeks him; it is good to wait quietly for the salvation of the Lord. Sit alone in silence.

Hope

God watches over us like a loving Father, and if we trust in Him, He will not disappoint. It is in silence He comes and speaks, it is in silence we can listen to the Holy Spirit, which resides in us.

May 9

Psalm 139:23-24

Search me O God and know my heart. Test me and know my thoughts. Point out anything in me that offends you. Lead me along the path of everlasting life.

Guidance

God knows our thoughts and our hearts. If our intentions are not good, He wants to correct them. He leads us lovingly, kindly, and honestly to a better life. He wants a good life for us, so when we feel nudged or gently guided to go His way instead of our own, follow His ways. They will lead to a full and everlasting life.

May 10

John 14:6-8

Jesus answered, "I am the way the truth and the life. No one comes to the Father except through me. If you really know me you will know my Father as well. From now on, you do know him and have seen him."

Knowledge

Jesus leads us to the Father. If we know Jesus, we know the way, the truth, and the life. He is one with God, so to know Jesus is to know God, and to know God is to accept His son Jesus into your life. They are one and to know them intimately will transform your life.

May 11

Ephesians 4:32

Be kind and compassionate to one another, forgiving each other, just as in Christ, God forgave you.

Love

We are called to forgive, even when our hearts are hardened towards the person who hurt us. God is a God of compassion and love. He wants us to open our hearts in forgiveness, and when we do, we open ourselves to an understanding—a truth or insight we have never had before. And in turn, there is healing for our hearts.

May 12

Romans 12:2

Do not conform to the pattern of this world, but be transformed by the renewing of your mind. Then you will be able to test and approve what God's will is, his good and pleasing perfect will.

Guidance

God has a plan for what He wants in our lives. When we seek to let go of our will and seek to do His, we see that He loves us and created us for a purpose. When we realize this, we are transformed and eager to see that it is fulfilled.

May 13

Matthew 5:48

Be perfect, therefore, as your heavenly Father is perfect.

Obedience

God is perfect in every way. He asks us to strive to be like Him. Strive to be loving, strive to be at peace, strive to be patient, strive to do good things with a loving heart. We are made in His image and He loves us.

May 14

Matthew 13: 36-43

Then he left the crowd and went into the house. His disciples came to him and said, "Explain the parable of the weeds of the field."

He answered, "The one who sowed the good seed is the Son of Man. The field is the world, and the good seed stands for the people of the kingdom. The weeds are the people of the evil one, and the enemy who sows them is the devil. The harvest is the end of the age. The Son of man sends out his angels, and they will weed out of his kingdom everything that causes sin and all who do evil. They will throw them into the blazing furnace where there will be weeping and gnashing of teeth. Then the righteous will shine like the sun in the kingdom of their Father. Whoever has ears let them hear.

Protection

God knows His people. He loves them and will protect them. He watches over us both day and night, both Him and his angels. We are the good seed that he plants on this earth, to spread goodness throughout. He loves us, and when we feel this love we can shine our light like the sun for others to see.

May 15

Acts 2:28

You have made known to me the paths of life; you will fill me with joy in your presence.

Guidance

God will instruct us on the way we should go, but we need to listen. He speaks to us in many different ways: through a gentle whisper, through others, or through the unfolding of the day, which can seem heavenly. Ultimately, we need to open our hearts and our minds to what He is telling us. His ways, His life for us, lead us to joy.

May 16

Luke 2:52

And Jesus grew, in wisdom and stature, and in favor with God and man.

Obedience

Jesus grew to be wise and upright and both God and man looked at him with admiration and love. God wants the same for us, to be good people that others respect, love and admire; true followers of Jesus.

May 17

John 10:7-10

"Very truly I tell you, I am the gate for the sheep. All who have come before me are thieves and robbers, but the sheep have not listened to them. I am the gate; whoever enters through me will be saved. They will come in and go out and find pasture. The thief comes only to steal, and kill and destroy; I have come that they may have life to the full.

Protection

Jesus is our shepherd and we are his sheep. He watches over us, protects us, and wants the best for us. He did not come to punish or condemn us, but to bring us to fullness of joy and peace. A life with him leads exactly to that.

May 18

Ephesians 6:10-17

Finally be strong in the Lord and in his mighty power. Put on the full armor of God, so that you can take your stand against the devil's schemes. For our struggle is not against flesh and blood, but against rulers, against authorities, against the powers of the dark world and against the spiritual forces of evil in the heavenly realms. Therefore put on the full armor of God, so that when the day of evil comes, you may be able to stand your ground, and after you have done everything, to stand firm, with the belt of truth buckled around your waist, with the breastplate of righteousness in place and with your feet fitted with the readiness that comes from the gospel of peace. In addition to all this, take up the shield of faith, with which you can extinguish all the flaming arrows of the evil one. Take the helmet of salvation and the sword of the Spirit which is the word of God.

Protection

God is our protector, but we need to battle evil with the resources that He gives us to do so. The truth, scriptures, and His peace are all valuable tools to battle evil, armed with God at our side. Know that with God, we can triumph over all.

May 19

Psalm 116:1-2

I love the Lord for He heard my voice;

He heard me cry for mercy.

Because he turned his ear to me,

I will call on him as long as I live.

Guidance

It is with love and an open heart that we hear God's voice when we cry out to Him for our needs or for mercy. He listens to our pleas and knows our heart's desires. Be assured that we can turn to Him again and again.

May 20

Psalm 46:1-2

God is our refuge and our strength, our ever-present help in trouble.

Therefore we will not fear,

Though the earth give way

And the mountains fall into the sea

Protection

When you are troubled with doubts and fears, there is one place you can go to find refuge and safety, that is to God. Feel His loving arms around you, His strength to uphold you, and His calming presence help your worries subside.

May 21

Jeremiah 6:16

This is what the Lord says; stand at the crossroads and look;

Ask for the ancient paths,

Ask where the good way is,

And walk in it,

And you will find rest for your souls.

But you said, "we will walk not in it"

Guidance

God's guidance is wonderful and will help us, in whatever He calls us to do on this earth. When you come to a crossroads or need assistance along the way, pray. It is vital to pray, but what is more important is to listen. When we ask to be shown the way God will instruct us, and if it is the right way, it will be filled with peace, freedom, and rest for our souls.

May 22

Mark 6:30-31

The apostles gathered around Jesus and reported to him all they had done and taught. Then because so many people were coming and going that they did not even have a chance to eat, he said to them, "Come with me by yourselves to a quiet place and get some rest." So they went away by themselves in a boat to a solitary place.

Peace

God wants us to have peace and rest. Sometimes, we need to give ourselves a break from all activity and find a place we can rest. We don't always have to go to a destination; we can stop and attain that rest in our inward being through contemplation and resting in God. Whether we go to a solitary place within, or find a quiet place to get away, we know God will be there to meet us.

May 23

Colossians 3:23-24

Whatever you do, work at it with all your heart, as working for the Lord, not human masters, since you know that you will receive an inheritance from the Lord as a reward. It is the Lord Christ you are serving.

Obedience

We are to remain true and obedient to God's plan for us. He created us for a purpose, and when that is revealed, we must work toward that with all of our hearts. It is the Lord that we serve from that day on, and we will seek to do His will.

May 24

Matthew 16:24-28

Whoever wants to be my disciples must deny themselves and take up their cross and follow me. For whoever wants to save their life will lose it, but whoever loses their life for me will find it. What good will it be for someone to gain the whole world, yet forfeit their soul? For the Son of Man is going to come in his Father's glory with his angels, and then he will reward each person according to what they have done.

Obedience

Being faithful to God is giving up one's own desires, wants, and comfort, and instead following what God desires. It is not the earthly things that we must strive for, but the spiritual things in this life. We must deny our worldly ways and focus on God. His ways are truth, life, and love, and we will be rewarded.

May 25

Isaiah 60:1

Arise, shine, for your light has come, and the glory of the Lord rises upon you.

Joy

When God is with us, and in us, we are a light to all, and God's glory and goodness abound. We are to be that light to others—the same light that God is to us—and shine bright to bring forth God's love into this world.

May 26

John 16:33

I have told you these things, so that in me you may have peace. In this world, you will have trouble. But take heart, I have overcome the world.

Peace

Jesus does not promise us a life without trouble or care, but he does promise that he will be with us through it all, and will give us his peace. His peace surpasses all understanding and will remain in our hearts forever.

May 27

Hebrews 11:1

Now faith is confidence in what we hope for and assurance about what we do not see.

Faith

Faith is trusting that what we hope for will be granted and having great confidence that God is in control of it all. Take that leap of faith and know without a doubt that if it is what God wants for you, He will bless you.

May 28

Philippians 2:5-11

In your relationship with one another, have the same mindset as Christ Jesus: Who being in very nature God, did not consider equality with God something to be used to his own advantage; rather, he made himself nothing by taking the very nature of a servant, being made in human likeness, and being found in appearance as a man, he humbled himself by becoming obedient to death – even death on a cross. Therefore God exalted him to the highest place and gave him the name that is above every other name, that at the name Jesus every knee should bow, in heaven and under the earth and every tongue acknowledge that Jesus Christ is Lord, to the glory of God the Father.

Humility

Jesus walked on this earth in humility, and gave love, and was loved. He did not exalt himself, but lived a very humble life and was a servant of all. We are to imitate Jesus, and think of others above ourselves, and take on the heart of Christ.

May 29

John 1:1-5

In the beginning was the Word, and the Word was with God, and Word was God. He was with God in the beginning. Through him all things were made; without him nothing was made that had been made. In him was life, and that life was the light of all mankind. The light shines in the darkness, and the darkness has not overcome it.

Knowledge

We know God created everything and all that He created is good. That does not mean there is no darkness in the world; but God is light, and that light can never be overcome. His light shines through in our difficulties, in our challenges, and in all of our sorrow.

May 30

John 6: 48-51

I am the bread of life. Your ancestors ate the manna in the wilderness, yet they died. But here is the bread that comes down from heaven, which anyone may eat and not die. I am the living bread that came down from heaven. Whoever eats this bread will live forever. This bread is my flesh, which I will give for the life of the world.

Hope

Jesus is the bread of life, and he came to give us life on this earth and beyond. When we eat his body, we are sustained with life and the ability to help others and serve him. His body, his blood, gives us life on this earth, and one day in his kingdom of heaven.

May 31

Isaiah 64:8

Yet you are our Father. We are the clay, you are the potter; we are all the work of your hand.

Guidance

God is constantly shaping us and molding us. We are His creation and we are all special in His eyes. He is forming us, both inside and out, to be pure beauty, joy, and love. He is our Creator and we are His creation.

June 1

Hebrews 10:23

Let us hold unswervingly to the hope we profess, for he who promised is faithful.

Hope

We hope for many things, but the things that God has planted in our hearts to hope for are the things He will not fail to give us. God places in our hearts our hopes, our dreams, and our prayers, as well as what He wants for our lives. Hold on to these and remain faithful.

June 2

Luke 14:11

For all who exalt themselves will be humbled and those who humble themselves will be exalted.

Humility

Humility is not showing weakness, but freeing ourselves of our own pride and ego, and depending on God for everything. It is when we rely on the Lord, and not ourselves, that we will be transformed into a new person—one who loves and is love, and one who is in beautiful union with God.

June 3

Luke 17:20-21

Once on being asked by the Pharisees when the kingdom of God would come, Jesus replied, "The coming of the kingdom of God is not something that can be observed, nor will people say, "Here it is" or "There it is" because the kingdom of God is within you.

Love

We don't need to look to the future for the kingdom of God, or strive at some point to obtain it, because the kingdom of God is right here, right now. We are to care for others here on this earth and to be a beacon of God's light. The kingdom of God is in our hearts, minds, hands, and soul.

June 4

Philippians 2:1-4

Therefore if you have any encouragement from being united with Christ, if any comfort from his love, if any common sharing in the Spirit, if any tenderness and compassion by being like-minded, having the same love, being one in spirit and of one mind. Do nothing out of selfish ambition or vain conceit. Rather in humility value others above yourselves, not looking to your own interests but each of you to the interests of others.

Humility

To think of others before ourselves and our own needs, is the way Jesus wants us to live. When we walk humbly, living a life like Christ lived while on this earth full of kindness, thoughtfulness, humility, and love; that is the way of Jesus.

June 5

Matthew 7:13-14

Enter through the narrow gate. For wide is the gate and broad is the road that leads to destruction and many enter through it. But small is the gate and narrow the road that leads to life and only a few find it.

Obedience

The way of God is a road that many strive to follow. When we want to enter into doing God's will—to enter into that small gate—we may have a difficult time. But he keeps the gate open and he lights the narrow road ahead of us with His love. He never closes that gate because He wants us to come in. Enter through that narrow gate and experience a life of love, peace, joy, and happiness that only God can give.

June 6

Isaiah 32:17

The fruit of that righteousness will be peace, and its effect will be quietness and confidence forever.

Peace

When we do God's will and live a life that is pleasing to Him, we will have peace. In His love, there is a quiet confidence that is the essence of our being. When we are right with God, we are at peace with our Creator, and in turn, with all of His creation.

June 7

Psalm 34:8

Taste and see that the Lord is good; blessed is the one who takes refuge in him.

Protection

We see God's goodness all around us; it is so tangible and real. We see the good in people, places, creatures, and this beautiful earth. We know he protects us and that we can always find refuge in Him.

June 8

1 Peter 2:4-7

As you come to him, the living Stone – rejected by humans but chosen by God and precious to him – you also, like living stones, are being built into a spiritual house to be a holy priesthood, offering spiritual sacrifices acceptable to God through Jesus Christ. For in scripture it says:

"See, I lay a stone in Zion, a chosen and precious corner stone, and the one who trusts in him will never be put to shame." Now to you who believe this stone is precious. But to those who do not believe, the stone the builders rejected has become the corner stone."

Trust

We trust in God, and as we do, He builds in us a spiritual house, a temple, where others can come for His love, grace, and peace. His church and its people are the rock that stands steady, with God as its foundation, and it will not fall.

June 9

1 John 2:17

The world and its desires pass away, but whoever does the will of God lives forever.

Hope

We have one life on this earth. As we pass through this life, we need to make the most of it. God gave us this beautiful life—we need to cherish every moment and all the goodness it brings. We live forever knowing our eternal life in heaven awaits, where we will meet God in all His glory.

June 10

1 Peter 5:6-7

Humble yourselves, therefore, under God's mighty hand, that he may lift you up in due time. Cast all your anxiety on him because he cares for you.

Humility

God has a plan for you. When that is revealed, you must approach it with humility. Your life may not always go the way you think it should go, but that is when you need to trust and let God lead you, and cast aside any worries or doubts. He loves you and will ultimately see things through in the best way possible, always loving and protecting you along the way.

June 11

Isaiah 45:22

Turn to me and be saved, all you ends of the earth; for I am God, and there is no other.

Knowledge

We know God is there for us and we turn to Him completely for everything. He is our Creator, He is our refuge, He is our friend. He is above us, beside us, and guiding us, every step of the way.

June 12

Luke 10:2

He told them the harvest is plentiful but the workers are few. Ask the Lord of the harvest, therefore, to send out workers into his harvest field.

Obedience

When we hear God's voice and feel in our hearts that it is time for us to do His work, respond to His calling. He needs us, others need us, and there are few workers with much to get done. Don't ignore it or turn your heart away from it—instead, go towards your calling and you will be rewarded.

June 13

Romans 8:26-28

In the same way, the Spirit helps in our weakness. We do not know what we ought to pray for, but the Spirit himself intercedes for us through wordless groans. And he who searched our hearts knows the mind of the Spirit, because the Spirit intercedes for God's people in accordance with the will of God. And we know that in all things God works for the good of those who love him, who have been called according to his purpose.

Guidance

God guides us and helps us through the Spirit. When we have the Holy Spirit in us, we are led by God and God resides in us. There is no more striving to do our will, for now God is working in us and for us, and He will see to it that His will is accomplished.

June 14

Luke 10:27-28

He answered, "Love the Lord your God with all your heart and with all your soul and with all your strength and with all your mind and "Love your neighbor as yourself." You have answered correctly, Jesus replied, "Do this and you will live."

Love

We are called to love God so strongly, so surely, so instinctively, but that is not all whom we are called to love. We are called to love our neighbors, friends, and strangers—all who we meet. It is two-fold; as we intensely love God, and God gives us His love back, we can then share this love with others, a true gift from God.

June 15

Psalm 127:1

Unless the Lord builds the house,

the builders labor in vain.

Unless the Lord watches over the city,

the guards stand watch in vain.

Protection

We turn to the Lord for everything. With Him, all our work, labor, dwelling places, and relationships have that strong foundation. He is where we look to, and from our steady gaze on Him, everything else falls into place.

June 16

Genesis 2:2

By the seventh day God had finished the work he had been doing; so on the seventh day he rested from all his work.

Peace

God rested after his work was complete. God needed rest from all that He had done and we need that too. Work and rest: God desires for us to have both. In doing His work, you will be fulfilled; in resting, you will find joy, stillness, quiet, and peace.

June 17

Matthew 7:1-2

Do not judge, or you too will be judged. For in the same measure you use, it will be measured to you.

Humility

When someone hurts our feelings or wrongs us, it is easy to judge and not want to forgive. God wants us to forgive, to see the good in the other person, and to not judge. God forgives us, so we need to forgive others.

June 18

Luke 18:14

I tell you that this man, rather than the other went home justified before God. For all those who exalt themselves will be humbled, and those who humble themselves will be exalted.

Humility

God wants us to walk through life with humility, thinking of others before ourselves. This is how Jesus walked through life; being a servant instead of being served, never proud but always humble, thinking of others before himself. He selflessly gave of himself with abundant love, and we are to do the same.

June 19

Revelation 3:20

Here I am! I stand at the door and knock. If anyone hears my voice and opens the door, I will come in and eat with him, and he with me.

Obedience

Jesus is with us, in us, and around us. He knocks at the door, but it is up to us to let him into our lives. He wants to prepare a feast, a banquet, and share with us goodness and joy. Let us open the door to his love.

June 20

Ephesians 2:19-22

Consequently, you are no longer foreigners and strangers, but fellow citizens with God's people and also members of his household, built on the foundation of the apostles and the prophets, with Christ Jesus himself as the chief cornerstone. In him the whole building is joined together and rises to become a holy temple in the Lord. And in him you too are being built together to become a dwelling in which God lives by his Spirit.

Faith

We gather together as a family and the body of Christ in a holy building called a church, but the building is only one part of where we worship. The other part is in our bodies and souls. There, God comes to build a dwelling place in us where the Holy Spirit is alive. We can surely share that love and that Spirit with others wherever we are.

June 21

John 7:37-38

On the last and greatest day of the festival, Jesus stood and said in a loud voice, "Let anyone who is thirsty come to me and drink." Whoever believes in me, as scripture has said, rivers of living water will flow from within them.

Love

Jesus gives us his Spirit and love to live in us and flow through us to others. We are both grateful for and gracious with this gift, as it comes to all who believe. We are filled with this water which satisfies and fills us completely.

June 22

Philippians 4:8-9

Finally brothers and sisters, whatever is true, whatever is noble, whatever is right, whatever is pure, whatever is lovely, whatever is admirable—if anything is excellent or praiseworthy—think about such things. Whatever you have learned or received or heard from me or seen in me—put it into practice. And the God of peace will be with you.

Knowledge

God places in our hearts what is pure, true, and noble, and many other admirable virtues. We think of these and follow them during our day. We also listen to God's voice in the silence of our hearts. To put both of these practices into action—exemplifying these traits and listening to His calling—is what draws us close to Him and His peace.

June 23

Romans 12:9-13

Love must be sincere. Hate what is evil; cling to what is good. Be devoted to one another in love. Honor one another above yourselves. Never be lacking in zeal, but keep your spiritual fervor, serving the Lord. Be joyful in hope, patient in affliction, faithful in prayer. Share with the Lord's people who are in need, practice hospitality.

Guidance

God's guidance in all matters is vital. He gives us His words to live by, which give us hope and save us from our sins. He loves us and ultimately wants us to overcome all that keeps us from living a life of true freedom and happiness. It is time to listen, it is time to be there for others, and it is time to break through from whatever is keeping us from living a life with God.

June 24

Philippians 3:13-14

Brothers and sisters, I do not consider myself yet to have taken hold of it. But one thing I do: Forgetting what is behind and straining toward what is ahead, I press on toward the goal to win the prize for which God has called me heavenward in Christ Jesus.

Fortitude

Leaving our past, our troubles, our cares, behind, we push forward to what lies ahead: God's plans and future goals. We do not need to dwell on what is behind, but looking ahead, we see a new life, a risen life with Christ. We are blessed, because we see a life with Christ is a life that is full, rich, and wonderful.

June 25

Exodus:13:21-22

By day the Lord went ahead of them in a pillar of cloud to guide them on their way and by night in a pillar of fire to give them light, so that they could travel both day and night.

Guidance

The Lord lights our path by day, and leads us and illuminates our way. At night He does the same, so we do not walk in darkness when the Lord is on our side. He is a light to us always. We are never alone when God is in our lives and in our hearts.

June 26

Psalm118:24

The Lord has done it this very day; let us rejoice and be glad.

Joy

God wants us to find joy in every day that He gives us. There is always a way to find joy, even in sorrowful times. Look at the many blessings God surrounds us with and be thankful. A thankful heart is a gift back to God who gives us so much: life on this earth and all of His beautiful creation.

June 27

Ephesians 4:23

Put on the new self, created to be like God in true righteousness and holiness.

Love

When we let go of our old self, the one that holds us back from being true disciples of God; we can release our fears, doubts, anger, insecurities, or whatever that keeps us from God. Ask God to help you shed your old ways, and put on your new self, which is created in the image of God.

June 28

John 17:6-9

I have revealed you to those whom you gave me out of the world. They were yours; you gave them to me and they have obeyed your word. Now they know that everything you have given me came from you. For I gave them the words you gave me and they accepted them. They knew with certainty that I came from you, and they believed that you sent me. I pray for them. I am not praying for the world, but for those you have given me, for they are yours.

Protection

Just like Jesus was praying for and watching over his disciples, he does the same for us. He loves us—and as we follow his teachings and believe in him, he guards and protects us, too. We are his present-day disciples, and we are loved.

June 29

Proverbs 22:6

Start children off on the way they should go,

and even when they are old

they will not turn from it

Guidance

As parents, we love our children and guide them on their way. Teaching them respect for God, for their parents, for themselves, and for everyone, are important lessons to learn. Also, treating others with kindness, dignity, and compassion are Jesus's teachings and the way of God.

June 30

Jude 1:24

To him who is able to keep you from stumbling and to present you before his glorious presence without fault and with great joy – to the only God our Savior be glory, majesty, power and authority, through Jesus Christ, our Lord, before all ages, now and forevermore! Amen.

Protection

Even when we make mistakes and stumble, God is there to catch us or correct us in the way we are going. He is our compass and our guide, the very one who can get us back on track if we let Him. God wants us to succeed; He wants the very best for us, always.

July 1

Titus 3:4-7

But when the kindness and love of God our Savior appeared, he saved us, not because of righteous things we had done, but because of his mercy. He saved us through the washing of rebirth and renewal by the Holy Spirit, whom he poured out on us generously through Jesus Christ our Savior, so that, having been justified by his grace, we might become heirs having the hope of eternal life.

Love

Jesus shows us his mercy because he loves us. It is not by what we do that we gain this mercy, but by what we are, the children of God. And from that love he gives us the Holy Spirit, to live in us, renew us, and give us a new life.

July 2

Psalm 121:1

I lift up my eyes to the mountains –

Where does my help come from?

My help comes from the Lord, the maker of heaven and earth.

Hope

Look higher, as high as the mountains. Dream bigger and have your sights set on all God has planned for you to do. Keep moving forward, because God has good things in store for you and will help you to achieve them.

July 3

Luke 16:13

No one can serve two masters. Either you will hate the one and love the other, or you will be devoted to the one and despise the other. You cannot serve both God and money.

Obedience

Your loyalty and obedience to God means putting Him first in your life. You cannot serve both God and money. God is above all else, let money flow freely from what you do for God. He always provides for those who seek Him.

July 4

Jeremiah 7:23

But I gave you this command: Obey me, and I will be your God and you will be my people. Walk in obedience in all I command you, that it will go well with you.

Obedience

When we listen and hear God's voice, we know He is leading us and we move forward without fear to do His work. He reveals His will to us if we ask and are patient and wait. He is our God and will never lead us astray.

July 5

John 13:14-17

Now that I, your Lord and Teacher, have washed your feet, you also should wash one another's feet. I have set an example that you should do as I have done for you. Very truly I tell you, no servant is greater than his master, nor is a messenger greater than the one who sent him. Now that you know these things you will be blessed if you do them.

Humility

Jesus gave us a beautiful example of how he, the Son of God, was a humble servant and was ready to serve and think of others before himself. He washed his disciple's feet, a simple act, as evidence of this. When we think of helping others, putting their interests and well-being above ourselves, we are acting as disciples of Christ.

July 6

2 Corinthians 9:6-8

Remember this: Whoever sows sparingly will also reap sparingly, and whoever sows generously will also reap generously. Each of you should give what you decided in your heart to give, not reluctantly or under compulsion, for God loves a cheerful giver. And God is able to bless you abundantly, so that in all things in all times, having all that you need, you will abound in every good work.

Love

When we give abundantly from our heart, we will receive our just rewards. We may see how others benefit from our giving, yet at times we may never see how our giving affects someone. God sees and that is all that matters. When we give without expecting something back, that is true giving and gracious love.

July 7

1 John 1:1-5

In the beginning was the Word, and the Word was with God, and the word was God. Through him all things were made that has been made. In him was life, and that life was the light of all mankind. The light shines in the darkness, and the darkness has not overcome it.

Hope

God made all and is in all. His light shines on today and always through His people. The darkness in the world cannot dampen the light God so brightly illuminates in us. We are to be that light so others can see God exists and is present even today.

July 8

Ephesians 4:11-16

So Christ himself gave the apostles, the prophets, the evangelists, the pastors and teachers to equip his people for works of service, so that the body of Christ may be built up until we reach unity of faith and in the knowledge of the Son of God and become mature attaining to the whole measure of the fullness of Christ.

Then we will no longer be infants, tossed back and forth by the waves, and blown here and there by every wind of teaching and by the cunning and craftiness of people in their deceitful scheming. Instead, speaking the truth in love, we will grow to become in every respect, the mature body of him who is the head, that is Christ.

Knowledge

We know we are the people of a God who loves us, respects us, and keeps us under his care. With confidence, love, and trust, we move forward speaking the truth to people, also becoming mature Christians in our faith walk; loving, living, and caring for others along the way.

July 9

Colossians 2:6-7

So then just as you received Christ Jesus as Lord, continue to live your lives in him, rooted and built up in him, strengthened in the faith as you were taught, and overflowing with thankfulness.

Faith

We dig deep into the rich soil of our faith, a faith that nourishes us and helps us to grow. With this faith, we are able to love and serve others. We are thankful for Jesus our Lord who sustains us and enriches us with his love.

July 10

Isaiah 40:3-5

A voice of one calling in the wilderness, prepare the way for the Lord, make straight in the desert a highway for our God.

Every valley shall be raised up, every mountain and hill made low;

The rough ground shall become level,

The rugged places a plain.

And the glory of the Lord will be revealed, and all the people will see it together.

For the mouth of the Lord has spoken.

Guidance

God will reveal Himself through His words and through His Spirit. With His guidance, we will be able to navigate the most rugged terrain and climb the highest mountains. Even though we may not know where the road leads, we will find our way because He goes before us.

July 11

Matthew 18:10-14

What do you think? If a man owns a hundred sheep, and one of them wanders away, will he not leave the ninety-nine on the hills and go look for the one that wandered off? And if he finds it, truly I tell, you, he is happier about that one sheep than about the ninety-nine that did not wander off. In the same way your Father in heaven is not willing that any of these should perish.

Protection

Our Father in heaven is the Father of the lost, the lonely, the forgotten, and the ones that might wander. Nothing makes Him happier than bringing his lost sheep back into the fold. He is our shepherd and even though we may stray, He loves us and always welcomes us back.

July 12

Luke 8:16-18

No one lights a lamp and hides it in a clay jar or puts it under a bed. Instead, they put it on a stand, so that those who come in can see the light. For there is nothing hidden that will not be disclosed, and nothing concealed that will not be known or brought out into the open. Therefore consider carefully how you listen. Whoever has will be given more; whoever does not have, even what they think they have will be taken from them.

Joy

We are to be a light to the world and others will see the joy in us, which comes from living with God. This light cannot be hidden or concealed. What we give grows into something meaningful when we give to others without hesitation and with love.

July 13

Luke 2: 13-14

Suddenly a great company of the heavenly host appeared with the angel praising God and saying,

"Glory to God in the highest heaven, and on earth peace to those on whom his favor rests."

Peace

God watches over His people with love and showers them with peace. Peace is something to accept from God—it is God's gift to us. He gives it freely and it is wonderful to carry in our hearts. Accept God's peace, be grateful, and your life will change, as will the lives of others around you.

July 14

Matthew 1:18-22

This is how the birth of Jesus the Messiah came about: His mother Mary was pledged to be married to Joseph, but before they came together, she was found to be pregnant through the Holy Spirit. Because Joseph her husband was faithful to the law, and yet did not want to expose her to public disgrace, he had in mind to divorce her quietly.

But after he had considered this, an angel of the Lord appeared to him in a dream, and said, "Joseph son of David, do not be afraid to take Mary home as your wife, because what is conceived in her is from the Holy Spirit. She will give birth to a son, and you are to give him the name Jesus, because he will save people from their sins.

All this took place to fulfill what the Lord had said through the prophet. The virgin will conceive and give birth to a son, and they will call him Immanuel (which means "God with us.")

Faith

Jesus's birth is a beautiful story of joy, hope, and love, and we know God was with us on this earth in the form of His son Jesus. Jesus is still with us and in us through the gift of the Holy Spirit. Remembering that Jesus walked among us, and is still with us now, is important not only at Christmastime, but all year round.

July 15

John 14:27

Peace I leave with you; my peace I give you. I do not give to you as the world gives. Do not let your hearts be troubled and do not be afraid.

Peace

In our challenging moments, in our trying times, Jesus is there. We can feel his presence if we stop and be still. He comes to us in the quiet and speaks to our hearts. His peace is like no other and we will not be afraid.

July 16

Psalm 139:13-14

For you created my inmost being; you knit me together in my mother's womb. I praise you because I am fearfully made; your works are wonderful, I know that full well.

Love

We are all unique, intricate, beautiful creations of God, and are special in God's eyes because He made us. He created us for joy, He created us for purpose, He created us for love, and we know we are wonderfully made by Him in love.

July 17

Mark1:6-8

John wore clothing made of camel's hair with a leather belt around his waist, and he ate locusts and wild honey. And this was his message. After me comes the one more powerful than I, the straps of whose sandals I am not worthy to stoop down and untie. I baptize you with water, but he will baptize you with the Holy Spirit.

Humility

John the Baptist taught us about humility. We are to think of others above ourselves, but also be reverent to Jesus and our God who created us. When we walk through life humbly and lovingly, we are imitating John's way of life, and more importantly, the life of Jesus.

July 18

Matthew 19:26

Jesus looked at them and said, "With man this is impossible, but with God all things are possible"

Hope

God gives us hope, and He lets us know that all things are possible. All our dreams, aspirations and highest goals, can be achieved. Even when we are in doubt, we can place it in His hands and know that with God all things are possible.

July 19

1 John 2:17

The world and its desires pass away, but whoever does the will of God lives forever.

Obedience

The world and its desires are fleeting and cannot bring us true happiness, but what God desires of us will. If we carry out His vision, desires, and plans, we will not only be fulfilled; we will make a lasting impression on this earth. God blesses all those that do His will, and will reap His rewards.

July 20

John 3:16

For God so loved the world that he gave his one and only son, that whoever believes in him shall not perish but have eternal life.

Faith

We have not seen God but we believe, and we know without a doubt that God loves us. He gave us his one and only son, Jesus, so that we can know him and have eternal life in his kingdom of heaven.

July 21

Numbers 6:24-26

The Lord bless and keep you; the Lord make his face shine on you and be gracious to you; the Lord turn his face to you and give you peace.

Protection

God watches over us, His light shines upon us, and gives us peace. Graciously and with goodness, He surrounds us with love. In the stillness, we feel His love and we know that He is God.

July 22

John 1:32-34

Then John gave this testimony: "I saw the Spirit come down from heaven as a dove and remain on him. And I myself did not know him, but the one who sent me to baptize with water told me, "The man on whom you see the Spirit come down and remain is the one who will baptize with the Holy Spirit. I have seen and I testify that this is God's Chosen one.

Knowledge

We know that Jesus gives us the Holy Spirit and blesses us with this powerful gift. John testified to this, and we know without a doubt when we receive Jesus into our hearts that it is true.

July 23

1 John 3:23

And this is his command: to believe in the man of his son, Jesus Christ, and to love one another as he commanded us. The one who keeps God's commands lives in him, and he in them. And this is how we know that he lives in us: we know it by the Spirit he gave us.

Obedience

When we accept Jesus into our lives, he makes his home in us. The Holy Spirit comes to rest in us, in our very souls. We love and obey his commands for in them we find true happiness and our hearts are fulfilled.

July 24

Luke 2:11

Today in the town of David a Savior has been born to you; he is the Messiah, the Lord. This will be a sign to you: You will find a baby wrapped in cloths lying in a manger.

Humility

Jesus came quietly and sweetly, lying in a manger, for there was no room for him at the inn. That is how Jesus's life began, with true humility, and it ended with humility on a cross. Jesus came in the most ordinary circumstances, but was anything but ordinary as his disciples and the people that followed him found out, and we find out even today.

July 25

Mark 6:45-51

Immediately Jesus made his disciples get into the boat and go ahead of him to Bethsaida, while he dismissed the crowd. After leaving them, he went up to the mountain to pray.

Later that night the boat was in the middle of the lake, and he was along on land. He saw the disciples straining at the oars, because the wind was against them. Shortly before dawn he went out to them walking on the lake. He was about to pass by them, but when they saw him walking on the lake they thought he was a ghost. They cried out, because they saw him and were terrified.

Immediately he spoke to them and said, "Take courage! It is I. Don't be afraid." Then he climbed into the boat with them, and the wind died down.

Protection

Jesus will be there to calm the turbulent waters in our lives. If we really need it, he will come right into our life and be there beside us during difficult times. His presence in our lives gives us security and assurance that he loves us and watches over us always.

July 26

1 John 5-7

This is the message we have heard from him and declare to you: God is light; in him there is no darkness at all. If we claim to have fellowship with him and yet walk in darkness, we lie and do not live the truth. But if we walk in the light, as he is the light, we have fellowship with one another, and the blood of Jesus, his Son, purifies us from sin.

Faith

We are given life through Jesus Christ—life on this earth and in heaven. We do not walk in darkness when we walk in his ways on this earth, we walk in the light. We can make our mark on this earth as Jesus's disciples by loving others, serving God, and listening to his word.

July 27

Matthew 3:16-17

As soon as Jesus was baptized, he went up out of the water. At that moment heaven was opened, and he saw the Spirit of God descending like a dove and alighting on him. And a voice from heaven said, "This is my Son, whom I love, with him I am well pleased."

Love

God loves us. We are His sons and daughters, and He is pleased with His creation. He looked upon Jesus and told the world He loved him. God wants to look at us with that same love and tenderness and tell us the same.

July 28

Song of Songs 2:6

His left arm is under my head, and his right arm embraces me.

Love

The Lord cradles us and supports us with one arm. His other arm protects us and shields us from harm. All this in a loving embrace that comforts us both day and night. He is our comforter, our shield and our protector.

July 29

Matthew 19:21

If you want to be perfect, go sell your possessions and give to the poor, and you will have treasure in heaven. Then come follow me.

Obedience

Our worldly possessions are nothing compared to what is important in life, which is following Jesus and loving the people he puts in our lives. He wants us to give of our treasure, our time, and our talents, and then follow Jesus wherever he leads, for that is where our true happiness lies.

July 30

2 Timothy 4:7-8

I have fought the good fight, I have finished the race, I have kept the faith. Now there is in store for me the crown of righteousness, which the Lord, the righteous Judge, will award to me on that day – and not only to me, but also to all who have longed for his appearing.

Faith

Whether we are someone who is strong in their faith, or someone who sometimes doubts, God is cheering us on, wanting us to fight the good fight and finish the race. Let us do what we need to keep the faith here on earth, and one day when this life has passed, God will meet us in Heaven, His glorious dwelling place and heavenly home.

July 31

Romans 10:10

For it is with your heart that you believe and are justified, and it is with your mouth that you profess your faith and are saved.

Faith

It is not enough to believe. Jesus wants us to spread the word about our faith, like he did on this earth. That is our calling, to be his disciples, not only sharing our faith, but our love. If Jesus is at the center of our beings, this will come without effort but with ease.

August 1

Hebrews 13:8

Jesus Christ is the same yesterday, today and forever.

Fortitude

In our ever-changing world, we can look to our Lord Jesus for his steadfast love and devotion to us, his beloved. In both the good times and the bad, Jesus is true to his followers, and remains our rock and salvation until the end.

August 2

Deuteronomy 33:27

The eternal God is your refuge, and underneath are the everlasting arms. He will drive out your enemies before you, saying "Destroy them."

Protection

God is our safety and security; we are at rest when we are in His arms. No fear or evil can come to us when we realize He loves us and protects us. Ask the Lord to be your strength and your refuge, and He will.

August 3

John 13:6-8

He came to Simon Peter, who said to him, "Lord, are you going to wash my feet?

Jesus replied, "You do not realize now what I am doing, but later you will understand."

"No," said Peter, "you shall never wash my feet."

Jesus answered, "Unless I wash you, you have no part of me."

Humility

Jesus earnestly wants to be in our lives, and until we accept that, he stands at the door knocking, waiting to come in. He shows us what it means to love and to be a servant of others, because he demonstrated it first hand to his disciples. He wants to be a part of our lives and by our humble service help others grow closer to him.

August 4

Psalm 18:1

I love you Lord, my strength.

Fortitude

God is our strength and our refuge, we turn to Him in weakness, and He is always there. He is our rock and our fortress to protect us from evil, and watch over us both day and night.

August 5

Mark 4: 30-32

Again he said, "What shall we say the kingdom of God is like, or what parable shall we describe it?" It is like a mustard seed, which is the smallest of all seeds on earth. Yet when planted, it grows and becomes the largest of all garden plants, with such big branches that the birds can perch in its shade.

Faith

If we are like a mustard seed that grows by faith, to become that large plant that shelters, but most of all spreads it's branches out in love; then we have become the kingdom of God.

August 6

Romans 12:1

Therefore I urge you, brothers and sisters, in view of God's mercy, to offer your bodies as a living sacrifice, holy and pleasing to God – this is your true worship.

Obedience

As we move through this life, we are to offer ourselves—our bodies, our minds, our souls—to God. When we live for God, we are made into the person He created us to be. Our life is made complete when we give our life over to His love.

August 7

Hebrews 2:17-18

For this reason he had to be made like them, fully human in every way, in order that he might become a merciful and faithful high priest in service to God, and that he might make atonement for the sins of the people. Because he himself suffered when he was tempted, he is able to help those who are being tempted.

Fortitude

Jesus was tempted and he suffered, and understands our pain and suffering because of it. He is the one we can turn to in every temptation, in all our suffering, as one who understands and cares. Turn to Jesus in your time of need, he sees your humanity because he was human too.

August 8

Mark 6:34-35

When Jesus landed and saw a large crowd, he had compassion on them, because they were like sheep without a shepherd. So he began teaching them many things.

Guidance

Jesus watched over his beloved, and we are to do the same. Can we give people—friends, family, loved ones—the same type of compassion and care that Jesus gave to others? We are called to love but also to teach others about Jesus, sometimes by words, but more so by example.

August 9

Mark 6:54-56

As soon as they got off the boat, people recognized Jesus. They ran throughout that whole region and carried the sick on mats to wherever they heard he was. And whenever he went – villages, towns, and countryside – they placed the sick in marketplaces. They begged him to let them touch even the edge of his cloak, and all who touched it were healed.

Hope

Whether we reach out to Jesus for healing, or he heals us because he is merciful, Jesus is here in our midst. He wants us to be whole, healed, and joyful. He wants us to be fully alive because he created us for a precious life here on earth.

August 10

Mark 7:37

People were overwhelmed with amazement. "He has done everything well" they said. "He even makes the deaf hear and the mute speak."

Faith

Jesus performed many miracles, and cared and loved people enough to do so. He also said that if we believed, we could perform miracles on this earth. There are people on this earth that care so deeply about others, in their own way, they are making modern day miracles by bringing about beautiful change as they help others in need. Have a deep faith and be guided by Jesus to help and heal others.

August 11

1 Corinthians 2:9-10

However as it is written:

"What no eye has seen, what no ear has heard, and what no human mind has conceived" the things God has prepared for those who love him – these things God has revealed to us by his Spirit.

Hope

God always has our best interest in mind. He has a beautiful, joyous, and fulfilling life planned for those that seek, find, and most of all, love Him. We look to a bright future ahead, with God leading the way in love.

August 12

Matthew 28: 18-20

Then Jesus came to them and said, "All authority in heaven and earth has been given me. Therefore go and make disciples of all nations, baptizing them in the name of the Father and Son and the Holy Spirit, and teaching them to obey everything I have commanded you. And surely I am with you always, to the very end of the age.

Guidance

We are to be Jesus's disciples here on earth, bringing others into the fold and blessing them with The Father, Son, and Holy Spirit. It is how the church and our Christianity grows, by bringing others to Jesus and his teachings. He promises he will be there with us, helping us to do exactly that.

August 13

1. John 4:19

We love because he first loved us.

Love

We know how to love, because we receive love from God. When we fully accept God's infinite love, we are filled with the capacity to love and also the knowledge of how to love others. This is God's greatest gift to us, to know we are loved by Him.

August 14

James 2:14-17

What good is it, my brothers and sisters, if someone claims to have faith but has no deeds. Can such faith save them? Suppose a brother or sister is without clothes and daily food. If one of you says to them, "Go in peace, keep warm well fed, but does nothing about their physical needs, what good is it? In the same way, faith by itself, if it is not accompanied by action, is dead.

Faith

We desire a great faith, and if we obtain it, we can use it to help and serve others. Faith without works, or helping others in need, is useless. God gives us a beautiful faith to help our brothers and sisters in this world and bring them to Him. When we reach out to others in kindness, compassion, and love, we are not only sharing our faith but our hearts.

August 15

Matthew 6:43-48

You have heard it said, "Love your neighbor and hate your enemy. But I tell you, love your enemies and pray for those that persecute you, that you may be children of your Father in heaven. He causes his sun to rise on the evil and the good, and sends rain on the righteous and the unrighteous. If you love those who love you what reward will you get? Are not even the tax collectors doing that? And if you greet only your own people, what are you doing more than others? Do not even pagans do that? Be perfect, therefore even as your heavenly Father is perfect.

Obedience

We know we are not perfect, but we can strive every day to be more loving, kind, thoughtful, and caring to our neighbors, our family, and our friends. We need to love our enemies, and pray for others who might have hurt us. When we give love to others, especially to those who are difficult to love, we are aspiring to be more like our heavenly Father, who is love Himself.

August 16

Psalm 136:1-9

Give thanks to the Lord for he is good

His love endures forever

Give thanks to the God of gods

His love endures forever

Give thanks to the Lord of lords

His love endures forever

To him alone does great wonders

His love endures forever

Who spread out the earth upon the water,

His love endures forever

Who made the great lights

His love endures forever

The sun to govern the day

His love endures forever

The moon and stars to govern the night;

His love endures forever

Hope

God created all and is in all. The stars and the sky, the earth and the planets. He created us in His image so we share in His beauty too; He loves us, and His love endures forever.

August 17

Isaiah 49:16

See I have engraved you in the palms of my hands; your walls are ever before me.

Protection

God has got you in the palm of His hands. He is our protector and we are etched into His heart and He won't let go. Feel that safety and security, not only for yourself, but for the ones you love.

August 18

Isaiah 58:8-9

Then your light will break forth like the dawn,

And your healing will quickly appear;

Then your righteousness will go before you,

And the glory of the Lord will be your rear guard.

Then you will call and the Lord will answer;

You will cry for help,

And he will say: Here I am

Protection

The Lord, our God, wants to help us and guide us. He wants to show us the way. When we stumble through the darkness, if we listen and open our hearts, suddenly a light will break through. God will guide us if we listen, and tell us the way we should go.

August 19

Jeremiah 17:5-10

This is what the Lord says;

Cursed is the man who trusts in man,

Who draws strength from mere flesh

And whose heart turns away from the Lord.

That person will be like a bush in the wastelands;

They will not see prosperity when it comes.

They will dwell in the parched places of the desert,

In a salt land where no one lives.

But blessed is the one who trusts in the Lord,

Whose confidence is in Him.

They will be like a tree planted by water

That sends out its roots by the stream.

It does not fear when heat comes;

Its leaves are always green.

It has no worries in a year of drought

And never fails to bear fruit.

The heart is deceitful above all things

And beyond cure who can understand it?

I the Lord search the heart and examine the mind,

To reward each person according to their conduct,

According to what their deeds deserve.

Trust

We must trust in God wholly, in His plans, in His love. We are confident knowing He is working His ways here on earth. We gain strength and courage to follow Him faithfully, knowing He is a loving God, and we will blossom on this earth if we abide in His love.

August 20

Hebrews 3:15

"Today if you hear his voice, do not harden your hearts as you did in the rebellion."

Guidance

God speaks to our hearts, but our hearts and minds are not always open to listen. He oftentimes has clear instructions for our lives and the direction we should go, but because of worldly distractions, fears, and worries, we do not listen. Keep an open heart and an open mind to Him, and He will show you the way.

August 21

1 Corinthians 12:27-30

Now you are the body of Christ, and each one of you is a part of it. And God has placed in the church first of all apostles, second prophets, third teachers, then miracles, then gifts of healing, of helping, of guidance, and of different kinds of tongues. Are all apostles? Are all prophets? Are all teachers? Do all work miracles? Do all have gifts of healing? Do all speak tongues? Do all interpret? Now eagerly desire the greater gifts.

Faith

We are all the body of Christ when we come together and use our gifts for the common good. We share our faith together, but we also share our talents and gifts when we come together in prayer and love, to serve our God.

August 22

John 1:1-5

In the beginning was the word, and the word was with God, and the Word was God. He was with God in the beginning. Through him all things were made; without him nothing was made that has been made. In him was life, and that life was the light of all mankind. The light shines in the darkness, and the darkness has not overcome it.

Hope

God's light is a wonderful thing. Even though we sometimes face challenges and hardships, we know God is there during those times. Ask God for love and guidance, then listen to your heart and reach deep down into your soul. You will find God's life and light shining within.

August 23

Luke 18:10-13

Two men went up to the temple to pray, one a Pharisee and one a tax collector. The Pharisee stood by himself and prayed. God, I thank you that I am not like the other people – robbers, evildoers, adulterers – or even like this tax collector. I fast twice a week and give a tenth of all I get.

But the tax collector stood at a distance. He would not even look up to heaven, but beat his breast and said, "God have mercy on me a sinner."

Humility

Sometimes, we may think ourselves better than other people for whatever reason, but that is not what God thinks, that is not what God sees. We are all created equal in His eyes. When we walk humbly through life, thinking of others before ourselves, that is what pleases God, and where we find true peace.

August 24

Romans 5:1-5

Therefore, since we have been justified through faith, we have peace with God through our Lord Jesus Christ, through whom we have gained access by faith into this grace which we now stand. And we boast in the hope of the glory of God. Not only so, but we also glory in our sufferings, because we know that suffering produces perseverance; perseverance, character; and character hope. And hope does not put us to shame, because God's love has been poured out into our hearts through the Holy Spirit, who has been given to us.

Hope

Everyone in life will go through trials. They are what shape us and make us who we are today. In big and small trials, we will persevere with God at our side. He guides us, loves us, and gives us strength through difficult times. From our own trials and tribulations, we can give others hope—that same hope we received from God and the Holy Spirit. It is in hope we persevere; it is in hope we will prevail.

August 25

Genesis 1:27

So God created mankind in his own image, in the image of God he created them; male and female he created them.

Love

God created us like Himself: good, pure, loving, kind, and joyful. God made you like Himself, and God made others like Himself. See the God in you and see the God in others.

August 26

John 20:24-29

Now Thomas, one of the Twelve, was not with the disciples when Jesus came. So the other disciples told him, "We have seen the Lord."

But he said to them, "Unless I see the nail marks in his hands and put my finger where the nails were, and put my hand into his side I will not believe.

A week later his disciples were in the house again, and Thomas was with them. Though the doors were locked, Jesus came and stood among them and said, "Peace be with you!" Then he said to Thomas, "Put your finger here; see my hands. Reach out your hand and put it into my side. Stop doubting and believe. Thomas said to him, "My Lord and my God!" Then Jesus told him, "Because you have seen me, you have believed; blessed are those who have not seen and yet have believed.

Faith

How do we go about believing in a God we have not seen, have not touched, or have not heard? By faith, we believe. We see Him in the beauty around us; in the flowers, the trees, the people we love. He touches our heart with a warm glow, or an inspiring thought that sinks deep into our soul. We hear Him in a quiet whisper telling us He loves us, and do not lose faith, *I am here*. We know it is God, because who else meets us in that moment, when we need Him the most?

August 27

Psalm 27:4-5

One thing I ask from the Lord, this only do I seek:

That I may dwell in the house of the Lord

All the days of my life,

To gaze on the beauty of the Lord

And to seek him in his temple

For in the day of trouble

He will keep me safe in his dwelling;

He will hide me in the shelter of his sacred tent

And set me high upon a rock

Protection

Our place of worship—our church, the house of the Lord—is a sacred place where we can go to find true peace and joy. Whether we go to worship or just to pray, it is a place to meet God, to hear His word, and commune with our Lord.

August 28

John 20:21-22

Again Jesus said, "Peace be with you! As the Father has sent me, I am sending you. And with that he breathed on them and said, "Receive the Holy Spirit. If you forgive anyone's sins, their sins are forgiven; if you do not forgive them, they are not forgiven.

Peace

Peace with God begins with union with God. When we are moving, living, and breathing in God's love, we are at peace. Then we, just like the apostles, can go out into the world and spread God's love. He blesses us with the Holy Spirit, His presence in us, to go do exactly that.

August 29

Isaiah 54:10

Though the mountains be shaken

And the hills removed,

Yet my unfailing love for you will not be shaken

"Nor my covenant of peace be removed," says the Lord

Who has compassion on you.

Protection

When the world is falling apart around you, the God of peace, the God of strength, and the God of compassion is right by your side. His unfailing love will see you through. Let His peace and His grace wash over you, and His calm remain with you forever.

August 30

Exodus 3:14

God said to Moses, "I AM WHO I AM." This is what you are to say to the Israelites. "I AM sent me to you."

Knowledge

To know God is everything and in everything, is to know God as "I AM." He is the ultimate presence, here now and forever. When we surrender ourselves to both the amazing things in life, as well as the challenging moments, knowing He is there through it all, that is when we recognize God as "I AM."

August 31

Isaiah 41:10

So do not fear, for I am with you;

Do not be dismayed, for I am your God.

I will strengthen you and help you;

I will uphold you with my righteous right hand.

Protection

God is with us always. He is our great protector, and we can seek refuge in Him when we are faced with difficult circumstances or situations. He will be there to comfort us and to be our strength in time of weakness. Lean into His love and do not be afraid.

September 1

Isaiah 60:1

Arise shine for your light has come and the glory of the Lord rises upon you.

Hope

God gives us hope to guide us, inspire us, and to keep us living a glorious life. If there are days that we struggle, we know that one day a light will break through and we will arise in His glory and Spirit. A new energy will come over us with a renewed sense of peace.

September 2

Ephesians 2:4-5

But because of his great love for us, God, who is rich in mercy, made us alive with Christ even when we were dead in transgressions—it is by grace you have been saved.

Love

God gives us love so we can hold it in our hearts, but more importantly, so we can share it with others. He gives us mercy, so we know that because He forgives us, we must also forgive others. He gives us grace, so we know we are saved and have eternal life, a life that consists of never being separated from God, now or in His heavenly realms. And for this we are grateful.

September 3

Luke 24:28-31

As they approached the village to which they were going, Jesus continued on as if he were going farther. But they urged him strongly, "Stay with us, for it is nearly evening; the day is almost over. So he went in to stay with them.

When he was at the table with them, he took bread, gave thanks and broke it and began to give it to them. Then their eyes were opened and they recognized him, and he disappeared from their sight. They asked each other, "Were not our hearts burning within us while he talked to us on the road and opened Scriptures to us?"

Knowledge

Jesus wants us to open our eyes, our hearts, and our minds to him. He has much to say and wants us to learn of him, and take in all the knowledge and goodness he wants to impart on us, especially through the scriptures. Listening to Jesus through prayer and through his word is how we get to know him and love him.

September 4

John 6:53-59

Jesus said to them, "Very truly I tell you, unless you eat of the son of Man and drink his blood, you have no life in you. Whoever eats my flesh and drinks my blood has eternal life, and I will take him up at the last day. For my flesh is real food and my blood is real drink. Whoever eats my flesh and drinks my blood and remains in me and I in them. Just as the living Father sent me and I live because of the Father, so the one who feeds on me will live because of me. This the bread that came down from heaven. Your ancestors ate manna and died, but whoever feeds on this bread will live forever." He said while teaching in the synagogue of Capernaum.

Faith

Jesus came down from heaven and was sacrificed for us to save us from sin. He is the Lamb of God. To believe in him, and the bread and wine we receive is his body and blood, is to receive him into our body. When we do this, he lives and remains in us, and can embody our hearts, souls, and entire being.

September 5

Matthew 14: 27-32

But Jesus immediately said to them "Take courage it is I don't be afraid."

"Lord if it is you," Peter replies, "tell me to come to you on the water."

"Come," he said.

Then Peter got down out of the boat, walked on the water and came toward Jesus. But when he saw the wind, he was afraid, and beginning to sink, cried out, "Lord save me."

Immediately Jesus reached out his hand and caught him. "You of little faith," he said, "why did you doubt?"

And when they climbed into the boat, the wind died down. Then those who were in the boat worshipped him saying, "Truly you are the Son of God."

Faith

Jesus wants us to come to him for everything—for guidance, for healing, for protection, for love, for absolutely everything. When we come to him, we cannot doubt that he will give us what we need, when we need it. He is a giving Lord, who knows what we need even before we ask him.

September 6

Psalm 62:1-2

Truly my soul finds rest in God; my salvation comes from him.

Truly he is my rock and my salvation;

He is my fortress, I will never be shaken.

Protection

God loves us, and when we need to be in His shelter, we can come to Him and find rest and peace. He builds a wall of protection around us, and we know we are safe and secure in His presence and in His love.

September 7

1 Peter 4:8-11

Above all, love each other deeply, because love covers over a multitude of sins. Offer hospitality to one another without grumbling. Each of you should use whatever gift you have received to serve others, as faithful stewards of God's grace in various forms. If anyone speaks, they should do so as one who speaks the very words of God. If anyone serves, they should do so with the strength God provides, so that in all things God may be praised through Jesus Christ. To him be glory and power for ever and ever. Amen

Love

When we love the people in our lives, we need to do it wholeheartedly, showing our love and hospitality to everyone. It is a blessing when we can offer ourselves in the same way Jesus offered himself to the people he met: serving God with all his strength, speaking words of kindness and tenderness, and walking in purity and love.

September 8

James 4:6-7

But he gives us more grace. That is why scripture says:

"God opposes the proud but shows favor to the humble."

Submit yourselves, then, to God. Resist the devil and he will flee from you.

Humility

Walk humbly through life like Jesus did; God looks sweetly on those that do. Bring God into absolutely everything you do. In your highs and your lows, bring Him into your life. With His grace, He will watch over and protect you always.

September 9

1 Peter 1:8-9

Though you have not seen him, you love him, and even though you do not see him now you believe in him and are filled with an inexpressible joy for you are receiving the end results of your faith, the salvation of your souls.

Faith

We know and love Jesus even though we have not seen him. We know he resides in us and with us, and his love for us is immense. We feel that love, too, when we think of him, pray to him, and sit quietly in his presence. Our faith grounds us in knowing he is our Lord.

September 10

Psalm 3:3-5

But you, Lord, are a shield around me,

My glory, the One who lifts my head high.

I call out to the Lord, and he answers me from his holy mountain.

I lie down and sleep;

I awake again, because the Lord sustains me.

Protection

The Lord is our protector. He wraps his loving arms around us and shields us from harm. He watches over us both day and night. We wake up assured, knowing He is going to give us what we need to sustain us that day, and always.

September 11

Ephesians 2:10

For we are God's handiwork, created in Christ Jesus to do good works, which God prepared in advance for us to do.

Knowledge

God created us with certain skills, talents, and gifts that He intended us to use on this earth. We have a purpose, each one of us, and can make a difference by using what God gave us and how He made us, to contribute and bless the world we live in. We are all special in God's eyes.

September 12

John 21:15-17

When they had finished eating Jesus said to Simon Peter, "Simon son of John, do you love me more than these?"

"Yes, Lord," he said, "you know that I love you."

Jesus said, "Feed my lambs."

Again Jesus said, "Simon son of John do you love me?

He answered, "Yes Lord, you know that I love you."

Jesus said, "Take care of my sheep."

The third time he said to him, "Simon son of John, do you love me?"

Peter was hurt because Jesus asked him a third time, "Do you love me?"

He said, "Lord, you know all things; you know that I love you."

Obedience

Jesus tells us to take care of his sheep, meaning the people around us. He wants us to do so with all our heart, with all our souls, and with all our might. He speaks to us like He did to Peter, but are we listening? Are we seeing the needs of the people around us and responding to them? Listen to Jesus and follow your heart into action.

September 13

2 Corinthians 13:11

Finally, brothers and sisters, rejoice! Strive for full restoration, encourage one another, be of one mind, live in peace. And the God of love and peace will be with you.

Peace

When we live with one another in pure peace and unity, God is in our midst. We can feel His presence in those moments, showering us with His love. Peace will flow through us and around us, and make it a beautiful existence.

September 14

Philippians 1:9-10

And this is my prayer: that your love may abound more and more in knowledge and depth of insight, so that you may be able to discern what is best and may be pure and blameless for the day of Christ, filled with the fruit of righteousness that comes through Jesus Christ—to the glory and praise of God.

Love

When we need to make a change in ourselves or in the world, we start with love. Love gives us not only the ability to see what is right and what is wrong, but also gives us the heart and soul to make the change that is needed, with God's love in our midst.

September 15

Matthew 7:24-27

Therefore everyone who hears these words of mine and puts them into practice is like a wise man who built his house on the rock. The rain came down, the streams rose, and the winds blew and beat against the house; yet it did not fall, because it had its foundation on the rock. But everyone who hears these words of mine and does not put them into practice is like a foolish man who built his house on the sand. The rain came down, the streams rose, and the winds blew and beat against that house, and it fell with a great crash.

Fortitude

Your foundation, or what keeps you strong and steady, is the Lord. His words, His Spirit, His wisdom, His guidance; all help you to stand on solid ground. When the hard times come, you will have built your life on this foundation, this rock that helps you remain strong and steady, and you will not fall.

September 16

Matthew 22:36-40

Teacher, which is the greatest commandment in the Law?

Jesus replied, "Love the Lord your God with all your heart and with all your soul and with all your mind. This is the greatest commandment. And the second is like it: "Love your neighbor as yourself." All the Law and the Prophets hang on these two commandments.

Love

To love God first, wholeheartedly and soulfully, is very important, because this is where all love emanates from. The love you receive from God, you can share with others. The love of God that is so beautiful and immense, that overflows from your heart, is the love God intended for you.

September 17

Ephesians 4:2-6

Be completely humble and gentle; be patient, bearing with one another in love. Make every effort to keep the unity of the Spirit through the bond of peace. There is one body and one Spirit, just as you were called; one Lord, one faith; one baptism; one God and Father of all, who is over all and through all and in all.

Humility

To be humble, patient, and at peace with everyone is not an easy task, but something we are called to do. Jesus walked on this earth in complete humility, always thinking of others before himself, and loving others with his whole heart. This is what we are called to do, and with God's grace we can.

September 18

1 John 4:13-16

This is how we know that we live in him and he in us: He has given us of his Spirit. And we have seen and testify that the Father has sent his Son to be the Savior of the world. If anyone acknowledges that Jesus is the Son of God, God lives in them and they in God. And so we know and rely on the love God has for us.

God is love. Whoever lives in love lives in God, and God in them.

Love

God is love, and He gives us his Spirit to live in us and pour love into our hearts. In turn, we pour love out into the world. With the Holy Spirit, God is breathing His life, His beauty, and His soul into us; divine life and divine love, now ours to possess, now ours to give.

September 19

Matthew 10:29-32

Are not two sparrows sold for a penny? Yet not one of them will fall to the ground outside your Father's care. And even the very hairs of your head are numbered. So don't be afraid; you are worth more than many sparrows.

Protection

God loves us and created us to be special. We are created by Him and for Him. He created our physical bodies, but also created our persona, our soul. He truly watches over us and keeps us from harm, for we are His children and He is our Father.

September 20

Matthew 19:4-6

"Haven't you read," he replied, "that at the beginning the Creator 'made them male and female' and said, 'For this reason a man will leave his father and mother and be united to his wife, and the two will become one flesh.' So they are no longer two, but one flesh. Therefore what God has joined together, let no one separate."

Love

God created man for woman, and woman for man. The two will come together and be one, and this bond so strong, joined together in God's eyes, shall not be broken. If God remains at the center of this bond, it will be a blessed and beautiful union, and it will last a lifetime.

September 21

Revelation 21:6

He said to me: It is done. I am the Alpha and the Omega, the Beginning and the End. To the thirsty I will give water without cost from the spring of the water of life.

Hope

God is with us in the beginning, and in the end, and everything in between. Our lives unfold from childhood into old age, and through it all, God is watching over us. He loves us for who we are, and reigns over His beautiful creation.

September 22

John 3:30

He must become greater; I must become less.

Humility

When we let Jesus make his home in us, our thoughts, words, and actions become his, and he becomes central to our lives. He increases, his presence and holiness; and we decrease, our selfishness and our ego. We humbly accept that if we are going to do good things for him, that this is a blessing.

September 23

John 11:25-26

I am the resurrection and the life. The one who believes in me will live, even though they die, and whoever lives by believing in me will never die. Do you believe this?

Knowledge

The Lord tells us that belief in him means living with him forever, here on this earth and beyond in heaven. We will never die if we live in Christ. What solace to know we are his and will be with him forever, here on this earth and in his kingdom of heaven.

September 24

Romans 6:11-16

In the same way count yourselves dead to sin but alive to God in Christ Jesus. Therefore do not let sin reign in your mortal body so that you obey its evil desires. Do not offer any part of yourself to sin as an instrument of wickedness, but rather offer yourselves to God as those who have been brought from death to life; and offer every part of yourself as an instrument to righteousness, for sin shall no longer be your master, because you are not under the law, but under grace.

Obedience

Offer yourself to God and all that He wants for your life. Be obedient to His will, and in love and righteousness, offer your mind, body, and soul to Him. Leave sin, fear, doubt, and trepidation behind, and go forward boldly into the life He has planned for you.

September 25

Isaiah 41:10,13

So do not fear, for I am with you; do not be dismayed, for I am your God.

I will strengthen you and help you;

I will uphold you with my righteous hand.

For I am the Lord God who takes hold of your right hand

And says to you, Do not fear,

I will help you.

Protection

There are times in our lives that will prove more challenging than others. Those are the times we need to listen to God's voice telling us to not be afraid, *I will help you*. In times of trouble, we can reach out and He will take hold of us and lead us to safety, to solid and sacred ground. He loves us and wants to guide us, ground us, and shelter us—and He will.

September 26

Matthew 18:3-5

Truly I tell you, unless you change and become like little children, you will never enter the kingdom of heaven. Therefore, whoever takes the lowly position of this child is the greatest in the kingdom of heaven. And whoever welcomes one such child in my name welcomes me.

Humility

When we are like little children—pure, honest, joyous, and humble—we are exemplifying what it means to be a child of God. Jesus was the perfect example of this: pure innocence, never self-seeking, walking through life in complete humility, and showing to others what it is truly like to be a child of God.

September 27

Lamentations 3:22-24

Because of the Lord's great love we are not consumed, for his compassions never fail. They are new every morning; great is your faithfulness. I say to myself, "The Lord is my portion; therefore I will wait for him."

Protection

Our God is a compassionate God. We can get consumed with life's ups and downs, but who is watching over it all? God. Every morning and every night, He looks upon you with love and compassion, so wait on the Lord for He will deliver you from all your cares and troubles.

September 28

Psalm 104:30-31

When you send your Spirit, they are created and you renew the face of the earth.

May the glory of the Lord endure forever;

May the Lord rejoice in his works.

Joy

God's creation is beautiful; the earth, the sky, the water, and all people. Treasure what we have and let God renew the face of the earth. Let us treat it, and the creatures and people who inhabit it, with loving kindness, and let us renew the face of the earth together.

September 29

Acts 17:28

For in him we live and move and have our being. As some of your own poets have said, "We are his offspring."

Joy

As we live, move, and have our being with God, we move through life in a joyous and gracious manner. To have God at our center, His Spirit filling us with life and love, is to have freedom to be who God created us to be.

September 30

2 Timothy 1:7

For the Spirit God gave us does not make us timid, but gives us power, love and self-control.

Fortitude

When we live in God's love, we gain strength and power through the Spirit that lives in us. We stand on solid ground knowing we are not only guided by Him, but also loved by Him; through all our weakness, faults, and brokenness, He is there.

October 1

Matthew 21:21

Jesus replied, "Truly I tell you, if you have faith and do not doubt, not only can you do what was done to the fig tree, but also you can say to this mountain, "Go throw yourself into the sea," and it will be done. If you believe, you will receive whatever you ask in prayer.

Faith

Having a faith that could move mountains requires a big faith, and that is exactly what God wants us to have. If you have that faith—that strong, solid, "move mountains" faith—God will reward you, and give you what you ask for, just believe.

October 2

Nehemiah 8:10

Nehemiah said, "Go and enjoy choice food and sweet drinks, send some to those who have nothing prepared. This day is holy to our Lord. Do not grieve, for the joy of the Lord is your strength.

Joy

The Lord wants us to be joyous. He wants us to give Him all that troubles us or keeps us from doing His work. Give Him your sorrows, fears, doubts, anger, and pride, and He will replace them with all that is good. When He does, you will gain a strength and solitude knowing you are now living a life full of His goodness, right here on this earth.

October 3

Matthew 19:13-14

Then people brought little children to Jesus for him to place his hands on them and pray for them. But the disciples rebuked them.

Jesus said, "Let the little children come to me, and do not hinder them, for the kingdom of heaven belongs to such as these." When he had placed his hands on them, he went on from there.

Love

Jesus said the Kingdom of God belongs to the little children. Little children possess qualities that are admirable and worth possessing, and we are all children of our Father in heaven. To be trusting, pure, innocent, humble, joyous, and kind, are the qualities of a child that Jesus so adores.

October 4

Psalm 56:11

In God I trust and am not afraid.

What can man do to me.

Trust

Putting all of our trust in God is not easy, but it is necessary if we are to live a life free of fear. Can we place our lives, our will, our future into His hands and trust that everything will be all right? We can if in complete faith we turn it over to Him, and trust in a God that loves us.

October 5

John 20:11-17

Now Mary stood outside the tomb crying. As she wept, she bent over to look into the tomb, and saw two angels in white, seated where Jesus's body had been, one at the head and the other at the foot.

They asked her, "Woman, why are you crying?"

"They have taken my Lord away," she said, "and I don't know where they put him."

At this, she turned around and saw Jesus standing there but she didn't realize it was him.

He asked her, "Woman why are you crying? Who is it you're looking for?"

Thinking he was the gardener, she said, "Sir, if you have carried him away, tell me where you have put him."

Jesus said to her, "Mary."

She turned toward him and cried out in Aramaic, "Rabboni" which means "Teacher"

Jesus said, "Do not hold on to me, for I have not yet ascended to the Father. Go instead to my brothers and tell them, 'I am ascending to my Father and your Father, to my God and your God.' "

Faith

Our faith instills in us that Jesus needed to go to his Father in heaven, so that we can have him always through the Holy Spirit, living with us and in us. This was the ultimate sacrifice, as well as the beautiful gift that he gave us.

October 6

2 Samuel 22:29

You Lord, are my lamp; the Lord turns my darkness into light.

Hope

God will illuminate whatever situation you are going through with a whisper of encouragement, a hopeful thought, or a warm feeling deep down into your soul. Listen, pray, and open your heart to Him. You will prevail with God at your side; your strength, your rock, your fortress.

October 7

Psalm 103:1-5

Praise the Lord, my soul;

All my inmost being, praise his holy name.

Praise the Lord, my soul, and forget not all his benefits-

Who forgives all your sins

And heals your diseases,

Who redeems your life from the pit

And crowns you with love and compassion,

Who satisfies your desires with good things

So that your youth is renewed like the eagles.

Joy

God wants good things for you, for your life, and we praise Him for that. He wants to give you His love and compassion, but also the desires of your heart. He gave you those desires and if they are honest, true, and come from pure intent, He will fulfill them.

October 8

Matthew 23:39

For I tell you, you will not see me again until you say, "Blessed is he who comes in the name of the Lord."

Hope

There will be a day when we will meet Jesus face to face. We will glory in his presence and we will bask in his love, joy, and mercy. What a beautiful day that will be, and we will be blessed.

October 9

Galatians 2:20

I have been crucified with Christ and I no longer live, but Christ lives in me. The life I now live in the body, I live by faith in the Son of God, who loved me and gave himself for me.

Faith

Jesus died for us, and we give ourselves to him so he can live in us. When we no longer live only for ourselves, we can use our body, mind, soul, and spirit to do his work. We are then no longer living a life guided by our own desires, but guided by his.

October 10

Matthew 16:18

And I tell you that you are Peter and on this rock I will build my church, and the gates of Hades will not overcome it.

Faith

Christianity has stood the test of time, and through the years of battling conquests of many kinds, the church has prevailed. When Jesus summoned Peter to build his church, he had no intention of letting it fall. It is built on the rock and its foundation is strong, because its foundation is God.

October 11

1 John 5:2-4

This is how we know that we love the children of God: by loving God and carrying out his commands. In fact, this is love for God: to keep his commands. And his commands are not burdensome for everyone born of God overcomes the world. This is the victory that has overcome the world, even our faith.

Obedience

We can get to know God by learning about Him, praying to Him, and spending time in His presence; then we can carry out His commands willingly and wholeheartedly. His commands are easy and one of His commands is this; to love one another as He has loved us, the most beautiful command of all.

October 12

1 Peter 3:9-12

Do not repay evil with evil or insult with insult. On the contrary, repay evil with blessing, because to this you were called so that you may inherent a blessing. For, "Whoever would love life and see good days must keep their tongue from evil and their lips from deceitful speech. They must turn from evil and do good; they must seek peace and pursue it. For the eyes of the Lord are on the righteous and his ears attentive to their prayer, but the face of the Lord is against those who do evil."

Obedience

Seek peace and doing good in the face of evil. When we pursue truth, peace and kindness, instead of harsh words and criticism, evil will shrink away. God sees our pursuit of righteousness and He will bless us.

October 13

Psalm 130:5

I wait for the Lord, my whole being waits, and in his work I put my hope.

Hope

We wait for the Lord and our whole being is hopeful. We hope our aspirations are fulfilled, our lives are full of love, and that we live in the joy and wonder of all that God wants for us. Be open to those hopes, dreams, and life-giving moments, and know that God blesses those that hope and wait and believe in Him.

October 14

Psalm 65:11

You crown the year with your bounty, and your carts overflow with abundance.

Joy

God wants us to know that we are blessed. He wants to bless us every day and every year, and from His abundant blessings will come love as well as joy. Sometimes we need to wait and see how He is going to bless us, and as we wait, we are thankful.

October 15

Acts 3:16

By faith in the name of Jesus, this man whom you see and know was made strong. It is Jesus' name and the faith that comes through him that has completely healed him, as you can all see.

Faith

Jesus heals. He does his part, but we need to do ours. We need to have faith, pure and simple, that Jesus can heal us and others. Believe, have faith, and know that Jesus wants to heal all—and has the power to do so, if it is his will.

October 16

Exodus 14:14

The Lord will fight for you; you need only to be still.

Protection

When you are lost and lonely and you feel life is a struggle, call out to the Lord and then listen. He will come to your side and instruct you on what to do in your time of difficulty. He will not only fight for you but He will give you all of His love; listen to His words in your heart.

October 17

Psalm 29:11

The Lord gives strength to his people;

The Lord blesses his people with peace.

Peace

God gives us strength in our weakness. Turn to Him when your strength is waning, and you need His power and love to uphold you. He also gives us peace when our fears overcome us. Rely on Him for both strength and peace, two things that can get us through any difficult situation.

October 18

John 3:34

For the one whom God has sent speaks the words of God, for God gives the Spirit without limit.

Love

God gives us the Holy Spirit and gives it abundantly, and from this flows many blessings. Whether we ask God for love, guidance, fortitude, protection, or peace, He gives it and does not hold back. Ask and expect big things, and God will give you the Spirit. And your heart will overflow with goodness and love.

October 19

Psalm 139: 1-3

You have searched me, Lord and you know me.

You know when I sit and when I rise;

You perceive my thoughts from afar.

You discern my going out and my lying down;

You are familiar with all my ways.

Knowledge

God created you and therefore knows you intimately. He knows your thoughts, your hopes, and your dreams. He knows your coming and your goings. He is familiar with your ways because He made you in His image, which is a true blessing in itself.

October 20

Luke 18:1-8

Then Jesus told his disciples a parable to show them that they should always pray and not give up. He said: "In a certain town there was a judge who neither feared God nor cared what people thought. And there was a widow in that town who kept coming to him with the plea, "Grant me justice against my adversary.""

For some time he refused. But finally he said to himself, "Even though I don't fear God or care what people think, yet because this widow keeps bothering me, I will see that she gets justice, so that she won't come after me.

And the Lord said, "Listen to what the unjust judge says. And will not God bring about justice for his chosen ones who cry out to him day and night. Will he keep putting them off? I tell you, he will see that they get justice and quickly. However, when the Son of Man comes, will he find faith on this earth?

Faith

God wants us to be persistent in our prayers, but He also wants us to have faith in Him that He will answer them. He is a God who brings about justice and goodness to His chosen ones, whom He loves.

October 21

Romans 13:11

And do this, understanding the present time: The hour has already come for you to wake from your slumber, because our salvation is nearer now than we first believed. The night is nearly over; the day is almost here. So let us put aside the deeds of darkness and put on the armor of light.

Obedience

Wake from your slumber and awaken to what God has in store for you on this earth. Do not delay this awakening, because in it holds your true potential. Everything that God is calling you to do resides deep in your innermost being, in your soul. Awaken to God's calling, and glory in the light and love that will follow.

October 22

Romans 14:11

It is written:

As surely as I live, says the Lord,

Every knee will bow before me;

Every tongue will acknowledge God.

Obedience

We humble ourselves before an awesome God; one who guides us, inspires us, and gives us His grace. We praise Him because we know He is the Creator of all, and His love and goodness reign down on us. We bow before the cross because Jesus saved us from our sins, and for that we are grateful.

October 23

Hebrews 12:14

Make every effort to live in peace with everyone and to be holy; without holiness no one will see the Lord.

Peace

Make every effort to live at peace with others. If at times you disagree with someone or are guiding a person back on the right track, do it with love and gentleness and an openness to their point of view. When you do, people will see the holiness in you and in turn see the holiness of God.

October 24

John 7:16-18

Jesus answered, "My teaching is not of my own. It comes from the one who sent me. Anyone who chooses to do the will of God will find out whether my teaching comes from God or whether I speak on my own. Whoever speaks on their own does so to gain personal glory, but he who seeks the glory of the one who sent him is a man of truth; there is nothing false about him.

Fortitude

God is teaching us and guiding us our whole lives. Do we listen to the word of God and Jesus's teachings or do we go our own way? Any person who decides that God's way is better, and that His words are meaningful and true, is a person who knows the truth. Be an example for others to see that God's way is the way to freedom and life.

October 25

Ecclesiastes 3:1-8

There is a time for everything, and a season for every activity under the heavens:

A time to be born and a time to die

A time to plant and a time to uproot

A time to kill and a time to heal

A time to tear down and a time to build

A time to weep and a time to laugh

A time to mourn and a time to dance

A time to scatter stones and a time to gather them

A time to embrace and a time to refrain from embracing

A time to search and a time to give up

A time to keep and a time to throw away

A time to fear and a time to mend

A time to be silent and a time to speak

A time to love and a time to hate

A time for war and a time for peace

Knowledge

Both in our lives and in the world, there is a time for everything under the heavens. God is in control of it all, the beginnings and the ends, the highs and the lows, and everything in between. There is a time for everything, so leave it in God's hands and you will find peace.

October 26

Proverbs 16:2-3

All a person's ways seem pure to them, but motives are weighed by the Lord. Commit to the Lord whatever you do, and he will establish your plans.

Obedience

God knows your true motives, because He knows your heart. If what you do or say to others is pure and good, it comes from a pure and good heart. Listen to your heart, but more importantly, listen to God. Follow His desires, because He ultimately has the right plans for you.

October 27

Matthew 7:7-8

Ask and it will be given to you; seek and you will find, knock and the door will be opened. For everyone who asks receives; he who seeks finds; and to him who knocks the door will be open.

Guidance

Sometimes you want to know the way that God is leading you, and you have a wondering heart. God wants you to ask Him for the way, and seek Him first. Then, doors will be open that unlock His wishes for you here on earth. Ask, seek, and knock, and you will know.

October 28

Luke 17:20-21

"The kingdom of God does not come with your careful observation, nor will people say, 'Here it is', or 'There it is', because the kingdom of God is in your midst.

Love

We bring the kingdom of God to everyone and everything by being God-filled people. Through our words, through our actions, through our very beings, we are the kingdom of God.

October 29

John 14:15-21

If you love me, keep my commands. And I will ask the Father, and he will give you another advocate to help you and be with you forever – the Spirit of truth. The world cannot accept him, because it neither sees him or knows him. But you know him, for he lives with you and will be in you. I will not leave you as orphans; I will come to you. Before long, the world will not see me anymore but you will see me. Because I live you will also live. On that day you will know that I am in the Father and you are in me, and I am in you. Whoever has my commands and keeps them is the one who loves me. The one who loves me will be loved by my Father, and I too will love them and show myself to them.

Guidance

The Lord gives us the Holy Spirit, to live in us and be with us. The Spirit is our guide and makes a home in us when we accept Jesus and God into our lives. If we are open to the Holy Spirit working in our lives, we will do great things on this earth.

October 30

Psalm 16:7-9

I will praise the Lord, who counsels me;

Even at night my heart instructs me.

I keep my eyes always on the Lord.

With him at my right hand, I will not be shaken.

Therefore my heart is glad and my tongue rejoices;

My body will also rest secure.

Peace

God guides our days and guards our nights. He never leaves us during either. If you need Him, just call out to Him, and He will come and give you the words of wisdom or the peace that you need. In His nearness, your body will rest secure in His love.

October 31

Psalm 55:22

Cast your cares on the Lord

And he will sustain you;

He will never let

The righteous be shaken

Protection

When burdens come and they are hard to bear, give them to God. He wants to take them and relieve you of all your cares. If we are following His words, His right and true life, we will not be shaken, and our hearts and souls will remain calm in His love.

November 1

John 11:40

Then Jesus said, "Did I not tell you that if you believe, you will see the glory of God.

Faith

God can and will do many good things in our lives if we believe. Let us always praise God and be thankful for all the beauty, healing, and goodness He brings to our lives, remembering He blesses us with it all.

November 2

Matthew 12:35-36

A good man brings good things out of the good stored up in him and an evil man brings evil things out of the evil things stored up in him. But I tell you that everyone will have to give account on the day of judgement for every empty word they have spoken. For by your words you will be acquitted, and by your words you will be condemned.

Knowledge

We know that if our heart is good, pure goodness comes out of us through our thoughts, words, and actions. If we have evil or malice in our hearts, then evil comes out through our thoughts, words, and actions. God sees, hears, and knows our hearts; be loving and kind to others and do not let other people's words and actions rule yours.

November 3

Job 22:22

Accept instruction from his mouth and lay up his words in your heart.

Obedience

God speaks to our hearts and souls through His words in scripture. It is in wonder and awe that we are still and listen to how God is speaking to us in those moments. When we do, we savor those words and keep them ever so gently in our hearts to help us in this ever-changing world.

November 4

Deuteronomy 6:6-7

These commandments that I give you today are to be on your hearts. Impress them on your children. Talk about them when you sit at home and when you walk along the road, when you lie down and when you get up.

Guidance

God's teachings—the wisdom He gives us—should be imparted to our children. When we talk about God, they learn and grow not only to be children of God, but Godly adults. It is then they will show you the time spent in prayer and teaching was not wasted, but was precious and will come back to you in blessings many times over.

November 5

Genesis 1:1

In the beginning God created the heavens and the earth.

Love

God created all and is in all. He created the heavens above and the earth where we dwell; the sky, the oceans, the earth, and the creatures and people who inhabit it. We can look at it all and feel immense power and love in His creation. Our hearts are filled with joy that we are part of this big beautiful world.

November 6

Romans 6:23

For the wages of sin is death, but the gift of God is eternal life in Christ Jesus our Lord.

Hope

When sin is a part of our life, we are not living the life God intended for us. Jesus came so we can have a beautiful joyous life not burdened by sin, but hopeful for a full life here and eternal life with Christ.

November 7

Hebrews 4: 14-16

Therefore, since we have a great high priest who has ascended into heaven, Jesus the Son of God, let us hold firmly to the faith we profess. For we do not have a high priest who is unable to emphasize with our weaknesses, but we have one who has been tempted in every way, just as we are—yet he did not sin. Let us then approach God's throne of grace with confidence, so that we may receive mercy and find grace to help us in our time of need.

Fortitude

Jesus went through every trial, every temptation, and every difficulty to know the journey we walk. He held strong and asks us to do the same. By his mercy, we are saved from our sins; by his grace, he gives us the fortitude and the strength to face any challenges that may come our way.

November 8

2 Timothy 2:22-25

Flee the evil desires of youth and pursue righteousness, faith, love and peace, along with those who call on the Lord out of a pure heart. Don't have anything to do with foolish arguments, because you know they produce quarrels. And the Lord's servant must not be quarrelsome but must be kind to everyone, able to teach, not resentful. Opponents must be gently instructed in the hope that God will grant them repentance leading them to the knowledge of the truth.

Peace

When we are at peace with God and ourselves, we do not want to fight with others, even when we are provoked. God does not want us to engage in foolish bickering or quarrels, but to be kind to each other. People can learn the attitude of peace by knowing that our loving hearts are pure and ruled by God, and their hearts can be ruled by God, too.

November 9

1 John 5:14-15

This is the confidence we have in approaching God: that if we ask anything according to his will, he hears us—whatever we ask—we know that we have what we asked of him.

Faith

When we approach God with our prayers and petitions, we place them at His feet, confident that if it be His will for us, He will grant it. We go to Him with love and an open heart, and if our prayers—either for ourselves or for others—are heard by God, we do not have to doubt or worry.

November 10

Mark 2:17

On hearing this Jesus said to them, "It is not the healthy who need a doctor, but the sick. I have not come to call the righteous, but sinners.

Guidance

Jesus came to help those that needed his help, his guidance, his forgiveness, and his mercy. Today, we are to lead sinners to him and his healing ways—yet, we are all sinners and at times we need his healing touch, too. What a blessing to have Jesus in our lives, who blesses us daily with his mercy and grace.

November 11

Mark 1:12-13

At once the spirit sent him out into the wilderness, and he was in the wilderness forty days being tempted by Satan. He was with the wild animals, and the angels attended to him.

Protection

Sometimes in life, we may feel like we are wandering through the wilderness, among wild animals. Difficulties may arise, but we know there is always God we can cry out to in the midst of our pain and suffering. He will send His angels to protect us. They may be heavenly angels, but they may be angels that walk among us: our friends, neighbors, and even strangers. Nevertheless, wherever or whoever they are, know that they are angels sent from God.

November 12

Luke 5:15

Yet news about him spread all the more, so that the crowds of people came to hear him and to be healed of their sicknesses. But Jesus often withdrew to lonely places and prayed.

Peace

Jesus went out into the crowds. He lived and breathed and moved among them. The people—and there were many—came to him for his healing touch. Yet after he was with them, he needed peace and withdrew to quiet places for rest and rejuvenation. We need to do the same. It is in this quiet solitude and prayer that we are made whole.

November 13

Psalm 42:1

As the deer pants for streams of water, so my soul pants for you my God.

Love

The deer thirsts for fresh, flowing water, and our soul searches and thirsts for God. We feel that longing, that desire, as we intimately draw near to Him. He is the one who fills our souls with our deepest desires, and He will fulfill them.

November 14

Isaiah 26:3

You will keep in perfect peace those whose minds are steadfast, because they trust in you.

Trust

Keeping our minds and hearts focused on God helps us to remain steady and grounded in God's love, instead of the distractions of life. When we trust in God's plans and His future for our lives, we are at peace knowing He is in control, and we can let go and settle into the beautiful life God has in store for us.

November 15

1 Peter 1:3-4

Praise be to God and Father of our Lord Jesus Christ! In his great mercy he has given us new birth into a living hope through the resurrection of Jesus Christ from the dead and into an inheritance that can never perish, spoil or fade. This inheritance is kept in heaven for you, who through faith are shielded by God's power until the coming of salvation that is ready to be revealed in the last time.

Hope

We know we are God's children and we will someday meet our Creator in heaven. For now, God shields us and keeps us protected, so we do not lose faith or have our faith shaken by this world or others around us. We are kept strong and faithful knowing He is our God and our hope is in Him.

November 16

1 Corinthians 10:31

So whatever you eat or drink or whatever you do, do it all for the glory of God.

Love

Our words, our actions—how we live our life and treat others—all reflect our relationship to God. If we are to do everything for His glory, we need to show it in all that we do. We are an example of what it means to live a life full of God's love, from loving ourselves to loving others.

November 17

Revelation 4:11

"You are worthy, our Lord and God,

To receive glory and honor and power,

For you created all things,

And by your will they were created

And have their being.

Knowledge

We know God created us, and everything in this world and the heavens above. We are grateful for this beautiful existence, because in Him we move, live, love, and have our being. To God we owe it all, and in praise and worship we thank Him.

November 18

Jeremiah 29:12

Then you will call on me and come and pray to me, and I will listen to you. You will see me and find me when you seek me with all your heart.

Protection

When you call out to the Lord, and genuinely seek Him with your entire heart, He will be there surrounding you with His love. He wants you to give all your cares to Him, and know you can place everything in His hands. God will come to you in your time of need, so pray and open yourself to His love.

November 19

1 John 1:9-10

Anyone who claims to be in the light but hates a brother and sister is still in the darkness. Anyone who loves their brother and sister lives in the light, and there is nothing in them to make them stumble.

Love

If you hold grudges, or carry hatred or resentment towards others for the wrongdoing they have committed against you, it hurts not only them, but you. When you carry those feelings with you, they tend to go deep into your heart, and your heart and soul cannot be open to receive all the love, joy and peace God wants for you. Forgive others as Jesus forgave others, and forgives you, and live in the light.

November 20

Psalm 34: 4-5

I sought the Lord, and he answered me;

He delivered me from all my fears.

Those who look to him are radiant;

Their faces are never covered with shame.

Protection

God is who we can turn to for all our worries and fears. When we come to Him in prayer, and we seek answers to our burdens, He will show us the path forward. Those who look to Him implicitly will radiate joy, because they have put their faith in Him.

November 21

Romans 12:17-18

Do not repay anyone evil for evil. Be careful to do what is right in the eyes of everyone. If it is possible, as far as it depends on you, live at peace with everyone.

Peace

Living at peace with everyone can seem like an impossibility, yet with God's help we can. When someone has angered you, do not show them anger. Just stop, breathe, pray and look at them through Jesus's eyes, and show them mercy and love instead.

November 22

Proverbs 22:11

One who loves a pure heart and who speaks with grace will have the king for a friend.

Love

Let us open our hearts and receive all the goodness God wants to give us. When we leave our hearts open to receiving love, joy, and peace and all the other fruits from God, we say no to having any evil reside there. And when our hearts are full of love, that love can be abundantly shared with others, which is one of the greatest gifts from God.

November 23

1 Corinthians 1:27

But God chose the foolish things of the world to shame the wise. God chose the weak things of the world to shame the strong.

Humility

When we are not trying to prove to others how smart, rich, and powerful we are, we can then walk humbly with God. Jesus walked on this earth in a kind, gracious and humble manner. We see his power not in force but by his love. We can imitate this love and humility in our lives too.

November 24

Matthew 17: 1-2

After six days Jesus took with him Peter, James, and John and led them up a high mountain by themselves. There he was transfigured before them. His face shone like the sun, and his clothes became white as the light.

Joy

Jesus wants us to give our life, our thoughts, our hearts and our souls to him, and then we will see him as Peter, James, and John did. Full of his light that shines upon us; he comes to us in all his glory, mercy and love. The joy that follows is an incredible gift that fills our hearts, until it is overflowing with his love.

November 25

Matthew 8:14-15

When Jesus came into Peter's house, he saw Peter's mother-in-law lying in bed with a fever. He touched her hand and the fever, left her, and she got up and began to wait on him.

Hope

Ask God for His healing touch, and He will show you His good favor. God wants to heal us and make us whole—physically, mentally, emotionally, and spiritually. He wants us to be healthy, strong, and at peace, so that we can do good works here on this earth, and live a joy filled life.

November 26

Ephesians 4: 25-27

Therefore each of you must put off falsehood and speak truthfully to your neighbor, for we are all members of one body. In your anger do not sin. Do not let the sun go down while you are still angry, and do not give the devil a foothold.

Guidance

If anger is in your heart, and there is a person or persons that have upset you, deal with it as quickly as possible. Do not let the sun go down on your anger as holding it in your heart brings you pain, as well as to others in your life. God wants you to wake up with a fresh clean slate every day, and a fresh clean heart and soul too.

November 27

Psalm 1: 1-3

Blessed is the one

Who does not walk in step

With the wicked

Or stand in the way that

Sinners take

Or sit in the company of mockers,

But whose delight is the law,

Of the Lord,

And who meditates on his law

Day and night.

That person is like a tree planted

By streams of water,

Which yields its fruit in season

And whose leaf does not wither –

Whatever they do prospers.

Obedience

God loves us and He blesses those that follow His teachings, His word, and His love. We will prosper when we follow God's ways, and yield fruit, fruit that will last.

November 28

Proverbs 2:1-8

My son, if you accept my words and store up my commands within you, turning your ear to wisdom and applying your heart to understanding – indeed, if you call out for insight and cry aloud for understanding, and if you look for it as for silver and search for treasure, then you will understand the fear of the Lord and find knowledge of God.

For the Lord gives wisdom; from his mouth comes knowledge and understanding. He holds success in store for the upright, he is a shield to those whose walk is blameless, for he guards the course of the just and protects the way of his faithful ones.

Guidance

God wants to give us His guidance, knowledge and protection. We know that if we search for His knowledge, we will find truth. If we search for His guidance, we will find hidden treasures revealed to us as we go through this life. In the end, He will not only protect us if we follow His paths, we will have much success, not as the world gives, but only as He can give.

November 29

Psalm 57:8

Awake, my soul!

Awake, harp and lyre!

I will awaken the dawn.

Joy

Upon awakening, we can immediately be aware of God in our hearts and souls; to start off the day joyful, grateful, and excited for all that He will bring us. Each day can be a blessing, if we greet God in the beginning of it and allow Him to be a part of our day.

November 30

James 1:16-18

Don't be deceived, my dear brothers and sisters. Every good and perfect gift is from above, coming down from the Father of the heavenly lights, who does not change like shifting shadows. He chose to give us birth through the word of truth, that we might be a kind of firstfruits of all he created.

Love

God wants to give us all that is good. He constantly watches over us, protects us, and gives His love and guidance through His word. He wants us to see the Christ in others and that others will see the Christ in us. A true gift from above of love on this earth.

December 1

Romans 1:17

For in the gospel the righteousness of God is revealed – a righteousness that is by faith from the first to the last, just as it is written: "The righteous will live by faith."

Faith

We are guided and inspired, and our faith is strengthened by the gospels and life of Jesus Christ. We are a righteous people; we live by truth, we seek justice, and see the basic goodness and dignity of all human beings. And because Jesus showed us mercy, we can show others that same mercy, with love and humility.

December 2

1 Thessalonians 5:14-15

And we urge you brothers and sisters, warn those who are idle and disruptive, encourage the disheartened, help the weak, be patient with everyone, make sure nobody pays back wrong for wrong, but always strive to do what is good for each other and for everyone else.

Peace

As we move through this life, God wants us to be kind, patient and good-hearted towards others. There are people in this life which make this easy to do, and there are people in our life that are more challenging to love. God says love them all, your friends and your enemies. It can be difficult, but it is in striving to do good that goodness will come. Be love in this world, and you will see love in this world.

December 3

Psalm 4:8

In peace I will lie down and sleep,

For you alone Lord,

Make me dwell in safety.

Protection

At night we lay our heads down to sleep, in the comfort of knowing God watches over us. Peace, rest, safety, and love are ours, with the Lord, our great protector, and angels surrounding us. Be at peace knowing we are in His loving care, always.

December 4

Mark 14:32

They went to a place called Gethsemane, and Jesus said to his disciples, "Sit here while I pray."

Obedience

There are times Jesus prays for us, when no words can come to us in our anguish, suffering, or pain. There are also times when Jesus prays in us, when we sit in silence and he reveals himself to us through his Spirit. Either way, we are grateful for Jesus's prayers, for us, in us, and around us, for they sustain us.

December 5

Deuteronomy 30:14

No, the word is very near you; it is in your mouth and in your heart so you may obey it.

Guidance

Reading the scriptures helps us to have God's words in our mouths, on our tongues, and in our hearts. Guidance from God comes when we take the time to read, study, and meditate on God's words and hold them in our hearts. From there, life blossoms, and moves us into action, as it helps us to share God's wisdom with others.

December 6

Colossians 3:15-17

Let the peace of Christ rule in your hearts, since as members of one body you were called to peace. And be thankful. Let the message of Christ dwell among you, richly as you teach and admonish one another with all the wisdom through psalms, hymns, and songs through the Spirit, singing to God with gratitude in your hearts. And whatever you do, whether in word or deed, do it all in the name of the Lord Jesus giving thanks to God the Father through him.

Joy

In everything we say or do in our life of serving God here on this earth, we are thankful. All praise goes to Him, our God who protects, loves, and walks with us on this earth, and to his son Jesus Christ. In the moments where God's love for us is seen, and in the moments that we cannot see Him, we are still thankful because we know He is there.

December 7

Romans 1:17

For in the gospel the righteousness of God is revealed – a righteousness that is by faith from first to last, just as it is written: "The righteous will live by faith."

Faith

In the gospels and in the scriptures, much is written to live a righteous life. When it says "the righteous will live by faith," we know that when we are following God's truths, Jesus's teachings, and the Holy Spirit's guidance, we are living by faith, and ultimately living a righteous life.

December 8

John 12:3

Then Mary took about a pint of nard, an expensive perfume, she poured it on Jesus's feet and wiped his feet with her hair. And the house was filled with the fragrance of the perfume.

Love

Mary's outpouring of love filled the room with a sweet essence, along with the perfume. When we are loving others as Mary loved Jesus during this selfless and caring act, we are leaving our sweet aroma wherever we go. This beauty and aroma will nourish the senses; an act of love that envelopes others in kindness and care.

December 9

Hebrews 11:6

And without faith it is impossible to please God, because anyone who comes to him must believe that he exists and that he rewards those who earnestly seek him.

Faith

When we believe with our whole heart that God exists—and not only exists, but is a loving and kind God that looks graciously upon those that believe—then we know we have faith. He rewards those that believe in Him with things that are important in life, such as surrounding us with people in our lives that love us and that we can love back.

December 10

Psalm 19:1-2

The heavens declare the glory of God;

The skies proclaim the work of his hands.

Day after day they pour forth speech;

Night after night they reveal knowledge.

Guidance

We look to the heavens above; there resides a gracious God watching over us. When we look to the skies and in silence revel in the beauty, we can sometimes hear God's voice in a whisper instructing us what to do, or just telling us He loves us. The thoughts and words come from God, but do we sit still enough to listen? If we do, He will touch our hearts. If we do, He will fill our souls.

December 11

Mark 1:15

The time has come, he said, "The kingdom of God has come near. Repent and believe the good news!"

Guidance

When Jesus says repent, he means change your direction, your thoughts, your actions, and where you are looking for happiness. Is God your source, the one who you turn to for all? Is God where you find your happiness, your satisfaction, and your ultimate contentment, or is it this world? Believe the good news that He is near, and believe the good news that He is here.

December 12

Philippians 1:6

Being confident of this, that he will carry it on to completion until the day of Jesus Christ.

Guidance

Our faith walk with God is a journey, not a destination. It is an ongoing and beautiful process where God loves us, shapes us, and transforms us into His likeness, if we let Him. It is a path of surrender and action all at the same time. As we walk this road, the road that leads to peace and contentment, we walk it knowing God is with us until the very end.

December 13

Luke 15:20

So he got up and went to his father.

But while he was still a long way off, his father saw him and was filled with compassion for him; he ran to his son, threw his arms around him and kissed him.

Love

In the Bible story of the prodigal son, the father not only welcomes his son back with open arms when the son has gone astray, he actually runs towards him and envelopes him with a hug and a kiss. That is what our Father, our God, does for us. He always welcomes us back, and will come to us with a warm embrace, if we stray or go too far from our home. And He is our home.

December 14

Proverbs 27:5-6

Better is an open rebuke than hidden love.

Words from a friend can be trusted,

But an enemy multiplies kisses.

Love

Being honest and open with someone, even if it means correcting them when you see them doing something wrong or going down a slippery slope, is alright if you do it from a place of love. Is your motivation correct? Is it a loving rebuke because you care about them? A friend tells the truth in a loving manner.

December 15

1 John 3:16-18

This is how we know what love is: Jesus Christ laid down his life for us. And we ought to lay down our lives for our brothers and sisters. If anyone has material possessions and sees a brother or sister in need but has no pity on them, how can the love of God be in that person? Dear children, let us not love with words or speech but with actions and truth.

Love

Love comes from the heart, and if we say we are Christians, but don't have the heart of Christ when dealing with others, are we really following Jesus? Christ gave of himself to everyone: the poor, the neglected, the weak, the humble, his family, and sinners. Do we give ourselves in love and action, or just in words?

December 16

John 11:40

Then Jesus said, "Did I not tell you that if you believe, you will see the glory of God."

Faith

If we believe, even when we doubt, worry, or lack understanding of our circumstances, we will see the glorious things God has in store for us. And through our belief in God, and by remaining calm and steady, we will help others to see that God is who we need to turn to in troubled times. In His own way and timing, He will always come through for us if we believe.

December 17

Leviticus 20:26

You are to be holy to me because I, the Lord, am holy, and I have set you apart from the nations to be my own.

Obedience

We are to be a holy people, like God, who is holy. Why do we need to be like God? Because then we are able to do His work here on earth. When we are like God, we are pure, kind, and loving. We walk through this earth as a servant and we bring others to Him, not only by our service, but by our love.

December 18

Luke 1:46-55

And Mary said:

My soul glorifies the Lord

And my spirit rejoices in God

my Savior,

for he has been mindful

of the humble state of his servant.

From now on generations will

call me blessed,

for the Mighty One has done

great things for me –

holy is his name.

His mercy extends to those who

fear him,

from generation to generation.

He has performed mighty deeds

with his arm;

he has scattered those who

are proud in their inmost thoughts.

He has brought down rulers

from their thrones

but has lifted up the humble.

He has filled the hungry with good things

but has sent the rich away empty.

He has helped his servant Israel,

remaining to be merciful

to Abraham and his descendants forever,

just as he promised our ancestors."

Humility

Mary was one of God's most faithful and humble servants. She was willing to give up everything to do what God asked of her. Mary knew being God's trusted one, she would be blessed. We know, too, that we will be blessed when we do what God asks of us, today and every day.

December 19

1 Samuel 3:10

The Lord came and stood there, calling as at the other times, "Samuel, Samuel!"

Then Samuel said, "Speak, for your servant is listening."

Obedience

Are we ready to be obedient when God calls upon us to serve Him, to follow a certain path, or when He is speaking to a certain issue in our lives? We can be ready, but the key is to listen. Are we listening to His voice? If so, He will tell you what His heart desires; just listen.

December 20

Proverbs 2:1-8

My son, if you accept my words and store up my commands within you,

Turning your ear to wisdom and applying your heart to understanding –

 indeed, if you call out for insight and cry aloud for understanding,

 and if you look for it as for silver and search for it as for hidden treasure,

then you will understand the fear of the Lord and find the knowledge of God.

For the Lord gives wisdom; from his mouth comes knowledge and understanding.

He holds success in store for the upright,

 he is a shield to those whose walk is blameless,

 for he guards the course of the just and protects the way of his faithful ones.

Knowledge

God gives us knowledge and understanding. He does not let us walk through this life blindly, but directs us if we ask. He guards and protects those He loves, who are faithful to Him. He loves us and shields us from harm, and wants us to live a beautiful life here on this earth.

December 21

James 4:10

Humble yourselves before the Lord, and he will lift you up.

Humility

Complete surrender to God's will, and walking humbly in his ways, is what God wants for us. He wants to raise us to new and soaring heights, but sometimes He needs to bring us to our knees to do so. Humble yourself before the Lord and you will be exalted.

December 22

John 11:32-35

When Mary reached the place where Jesus was and saw him, she fell at his feet and said, "Lord, if you had been here, my brother would not have died."

When Jesus saw her weeping, and the Jews who had come along with her also weeping, he was deeply moved in Spirit and troubled. "Where have you laid him," he asked.

"Come and see, Lord." they replied.

Jesus wept.

Love

Jesus in his humanity felt the sorrow, grief, and anguish of losing his good friend Lazarus. Because he shares in our humanity, and felt all the emotions we feel, we are able to call out to him in our suffering and know that we have a friend who is full of compassion. He will come to our side in our time of need; Jesus our friend, our Lord, and the giver of peace.

December 23

Joshua 1:9

Have I not commanded you? Be strong and courageous. Do not be afraid; do not be discouraged, for the Lord your God will be with you wherever you go.

Fortitude

God wants us to be strong, courageous, and to not be afraid. He needs us to be that way, because the things we are to accomplish for Him will not always be easy. But he promises us this: He is going to be right there beside us wherever we go. Knowing that He is our companion on the journey will make our load a little lighter.

December 24

Jude 1:24

To him who is able to keep you from stumbling and to present you before his glorious presence without fault and with great joy – to the only God our Savior be glory, majesty, power and authority, through Jesus Christ our Lord, before all ages, now and forevermore! Amen.

Guidance

Jesus is our guide, our rock, and the one who keeps us from stumbling. He helps us stand in front of God in purity and joy. He will always see us through, and in his love and mercy, will keep us strong and love us wholeheartedly for all of our lives.

December 25

Exodus 14:14

The Lord will fight for you; you need only to be still.

Protection

When you face a particular task, challenge, or crossroad in your life, God is who you can rely on. Listen to God and do your part, and He will do His. Pray that His will be done, then whatever the outcome is, you know it is from Him, because you prayed, listened, and surrendered to His will.

December 26

Micah 6:8

He has shown you, o mortal what is good.

And what does the Lord require of you?

To act justly and to love mercy

And to walk humbly with your God

Guidance

God's guidance is not only wonderful, it is simple in its requests. When dealing with others can we do so with fairness and justice? When others require our forgiveness, can we show them mercy? In the end, will we walk humbly through life, being an example of what it is to not boast or brag, and show love to others and to God.

December 27

Proverbs 3:9-10

Honor the Lord with your wealth, with the first fruits of all your crops; then your barns will be filled to overflowing, and your vats will brim over with new wine.

Obedience

God blesses us with riches that He wants us to share, and from that wealth we can graciously give to others. He wants us to give to those in need, and to give the first fruits of what we have, not just what we have leftover. God blesses those who give much and give freely.

December 28

Psalm 133:1

How good and pleasant it is when God's people live together in unity!

Love

We are God's beautiful creation and He intended that people of all races, creeds, and colors live together in God's perfect harmony. No one person is above another. No one person is more treasured in God's eyes than another. No one person is placed in higher stature than another; God created us all equal. When we live in God's love, and share that love with one another, we are living together in unity in God's beautiful creation here on earth.

December 29

Ecclesiastes 3:11

He has made everything beautiful in its time. He has also set eternity in the human heart, yet no one can fathom what God has done beginning to end.

Hope

God made all of creation—the people, the animals, and the earth—and it is beautiful. The things He made require effort to keep them beautiful. We need to take care of ourselves, others, and this planet to keep the beauty going. We realize this life is precious and goes on for eternity, because our hope is in God, who brings order and makes sense of our lives.

December 30

Matthew 14: 45-46

Again the kingdom of heaven is like a merchant looking for fine pearls. When he found one of great value, he sold everything he had and bought it.

Knowledge

We know the kingdom of heaven is precious and is of great value. Everything we do on earth is to attain it, and where is the kingdom of heaven? The kingdom of heaven is both in God's heavenly realms and here on earth. Make your life one of loving, serving, and graciously living a life of God's will for you, and you will spread God's kingdom here on earth.

December 31

1 Kings 19:11-12

The Lord said, "Go out and stand on the mountain in the presence of the Lord, for the Lord is about to pass by."

Then a great and powerful wind tore the mountains apart and shattered the rocks before the Lord, but the Lord was not in the wind. After the wind there was an earthquake, but the Lord was not in the earthquake. After the earthquake came a fire, but the Lord was not in the fire. And after the fire came a gentle whisper.

Guidance

God is here to guide us and tell us the path to follow; not in force or might or a thundering voice coming down from heaven, but in a gentle whisper. In both silence and listening, we hear His voice. It is a voice of love, strength, and power, and at the same time, a gentle whisper, guiding us and leading us home. And home is where God is.

Index

CPSIA information can be obtained
at www.ICGtesting.com
Printed in the USA
LVHW032128020323
740819LV00019B/116